R00446 16097

YO-AZH-126

FORM 125M

EDUCATION & PHILOSOPHY

The Chicago Public Library

Received_____ OCT 4 - 1985

TIME AND ITS USE
A Self-Management Guide for Teachers

TIME AND ITS USE
A Self-Management Guide for Teachers

CHARLES C. DRAWBAUGH
Rutgers University

TEACHERS COLLEGE PRESS
Teachers College, Columbia University
New York and London

To my wife, Ruth

Published by Teachers College Press, 1234 Amsterdam Avenue, New York, N.Y. 10027

Copyright © 1984 by Teachers College, Columbia University

All rights reserved. No part of this publication may be reproduced or transmitted in any form or by any means, electronic or mechanical, including photocopy, or any information storage and retrieval system, without permission from the publisher.

Library of Congress Cataloging in Publication Data

Drawbaugh, Charles C.
  Time and its use.

  Bibliography: p.
  Includes index.
  1. Teachers—Time management. I. Title.
LB2838.D73 1984   640'.43'024372   84-8578

ISBN 0-8077-2706-7

Manufactured in the United States of America

89 88 87 86 85 84   1 2 3 4 5 6

Contents

Introduction	vii
1. A Consciousness of the Dimension of Time	**1**
Characteristics of Time	1
Measurements of Time	4
Worth of Time	6
Sensitivity to Time	7
Uses of Time	9
Closing Statement	11
2. Managing Yourself	**12**
Assessment of Self	12
Goals, Objectives, Priorities	15
Managerial Tools	18
Making a Commitment	28
Closing Statement	29
3. Institutional Time Constraints and Bonuses	**30**
School Law	31
Local Board of Education Policy	33
The Teaching Contract	34
Job Description for Teacher	35
School Calendars	37
Daily Schedule, Class Schedule	40
Nonteaching Duties and Professional or Community Involvement	42
Leaves of Absence	44
Closing Statement	46
4. Effective Communication	**47**
Meetings	50
Communicating in Class	54
Reading	54

	Writing	57
	Listening	60
	Talking	62
	Closing Statement	64
5.	**Programming Activity**	**65**
	Planning	66
	Scheduling	70
	Closing Statement	74
6.	**Delegation**	**75**
	The Concept	75
	Why Delegate?	76
	Why Teachers Fail to Delegate	76
	How to Delegate	77
	Human Resources Available to Teachers	80
	What to Delegate	80
	Closing Statement	83
7.	**Saying Yes or No**	**85**
	Saying Yes	86
	Saying No	87
	Respect for Your Time	91
	Closing Statement	93
8.	**Wasting Time**	**94**
	Identifying Time-wasters	94
	Classroom Time-wasters	95
	Dealing with Time-wasters	95
	Procrastination	100
	Closing Statement	105
9.	**Time-savers**	**107**
	Doing the Right Things: Effectiveness	108
	Doing Things Right: Efficiency	108
	Twenty-one Time-savers	109
	Closing Statement	124
10.	**The Challenge**	**125**
	References	**129**
	Index	**133**

Introduction

Teachers are confronted with the awesome responsibility of teaching other people's children. Commonly they are also being burdened with an endless stream of demands, interruptions, and constraints from outside the classroom. Teachers are directly accountable not only to their students, but also to school administrators and indirectly to parents and the general citizenry. It seems that teachers are harried, beset, and put-upon by all kinds of people—who know their own rights and press their own demands. Thus, the teacher's load becomes a stressful overload that can and often does result in accelerated burnout, turnover, and early retirement within the ranks. The purpose of this book is to foil and actually reverse the unacceptable conditions just outlined.

This book was written to help teachers in particular but also other educators and professionals to get more of what they want out of both their professional and personal lives. Specifically, the author hopes to

- Increase your consciousness of time and your awareness of the preciousness of time as a human resource
- Provide an organized package of procedures, practices, and tips for you to use in learning to make better use of your time
- Promote skills and habits that will help you, as an educator, to become a more efficient and effective manager of instruction in school or you, as a professional to better manage the use of time in your life
- Inspire you to accept the challenge to put into practice managing *yourself* to invest more wisely in time

The book is designed to serve the reader as a practical self-management resource for learning about the dimension of time and how to use it to advantage. It is, in effect, a "how to" book liberally sprinkled with "why" explanations. Because teachers have excellent educational backgrounds, they are especially well equipped to apply the time use ideas presented here to their own particular situations.

A systems approach to time management is not attempted here. The complexity and diversity of individual minds, the incomprehensibleness of the dimension of time, and the heterogeneity of teaching positions negate a universal prescription or single model for managing oneself to use time more productively. In addition, the subject of time and its use is not an exacting science. Rather, it is an accumulation of facts and generalizations resulting from "experiencing" and tied together with strands of reasonableness taken from several disciplines. So in lieu of a systems approach, an organized body of concepts and practical suggestions is presented from which the reader may pick and choose when heartened to do so.

Chapter 1 is designed to develop your awareness of the dimension of time and your sensitivity to this omnipresent gift. Chapter 2 discusses the concept of managing *yourself* to use time, since time itself cannot be managed. In chapter 3, institutional time constraints in education are analyzed to establish the realistic limits within which teachers and administrators work. The first three chapters thus provide a frame of reference for the more specific, practical suggestions on using time effectively and efficiently that are presented in chapters 4 through 9. The final chapter challenges the reader to *do* something about what he or she has read—to take action to resolve the problems that prompted the reading of the book.

Viewed from another perspective, chapters 1 and 2 are equally applicable to educators and noneducators, since many of us need to become more aware of the role of time in our lives and of the possibility of learning to use our time more effectively. While chapters 3 through 9 are directed particularly to teachers, with an emphasis on public secondary education, public and private school teachers at all levels from kindergarten through college, school administrators, trainers in business and industry, and other professionals who experience the constant pressures of time can also gain immeasurably from chapters 4 through 9, which deal with effective communication, programming activity, delegation, saying yes and no, wasting time, and time-savers. The discussions are enriched throughout with illustrations, exercises, and forms for readers to use in assessing their own time use patterns and in learning new self-management techniques. The wealth of information about time use cuts across the many problems generally experienced among all levels and kinds of educators.

Introduction

The ideas in this book came from many sources. More than fifty books on the topic were reviewed, as were untold numbers of journal articles, research reports, and newspaper clippings. Naturally, the work was influenced by the discipline of agricultural education, the instructional expertise of the author, and peppered with a strong work ethic, a thread of his philosophy. The product represents a decade of gathering reference materials and conducting seminars on the topic and months of organizing the essence of both into this volume. A visiting professorship to teach a course on time management awarded the author by Texas A & M University launched the project. The priceless spin-offs of that experience were a full measure of satisfaction in doing the project and a profound respect for the resource of time.

May your rewards as a reader be even greater.

1
A Consciousness of the Dimension of Time

> Time itself is an inexorable force over which we have no physical control and about which we are quite ignorant.
> —Edwin B. Feldman

Characteristics of Time

The dimension of time is an abstract and theoretical concept. One cannot see, hear, feel, taste, or otherwise physically experience time. People say they know what time is, but upon further probing their explanations are limited and shallow, even though they live with time every minute and every hour of every day. The very nature of time is such that it is fathomless and mysterious even to the scholars who have pondered and studied it for generations.

The riddle of time eludes all understanding. Conjecture about it is often based on abstract thinking, and time is represented graphically in a number of ways. For example, time can be perceived simply as empty space to be filled with events and activities.

Time can also be conceived as moving in a cycle, in a coil-type pattern, or in a linear progression. The cyclic flow of time is represented in figure 1.1 as the movement from one season to another. While the figure depicts an annual cyclic flow of time, a daily cycle of time would consist of light, dusk, dark, and dawn. The concept of the

FIGURE 1.1. Cyclical Flow of Time

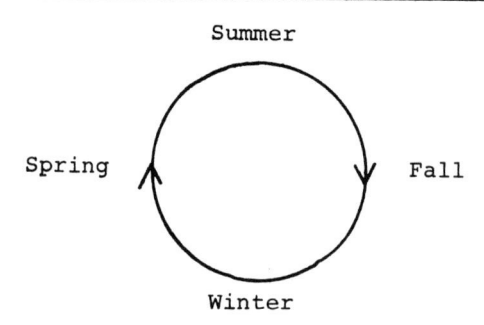

```
           Summer
            ___
           /   \
   Spring |     | Fall
           \___/
           Winter
```

cyclic flow of time, expressed by a closed circular line, suggests that time is recycled or reused. As represented by the circle, time has no beginning point, and it flows endlessly on a single plane in one direction.

The belief that "used time is gone forever" would suggest that time may flow in a coil-type pattern whereby the end of one cycle flows into the beginning of another. The concept of a coil-type flow of time is somewhere between the cyclic and the linear concepts and may be more plausible than either.

The linear flow of time, as presented in figure 1.2, is divided into the past, present, and future. The broken line is intended to indicate that no attempt is made to illustrate the amounts of time that are stored in the future or have flowed into the past.

The simple concepts offered here are not the only ones put forth for thought and discussion in the literature. The flow of time could be shown by lines running in many directions or by circles overlapping circles, for example, and reasonable defenses could be made for both ideas. It would be advantageous here to be able to reduce the several concepts into a single one to explain the flow of time. Since

FIGURE 1.2. Linear Flow of Time

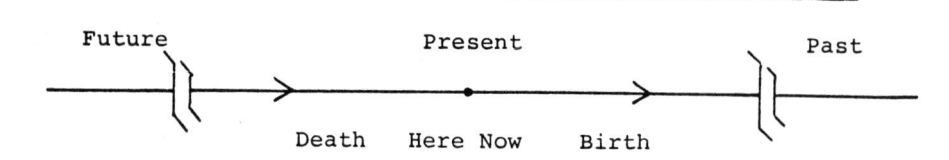

```
  Future              Present              Past
────┤├────→──────────•──────────→────┤├────
            Death  Here Now  Birth
```

that is an impossible task, perhaps the way to deal with the flow of time is to scale it down to a lifetime.

When a human lifetime or life line is superimposed on the linear time line, as in figure 1.2, the concept of the flow of time becomes more concrete. The flow of time precedes birth and continues after physical death. The life line is an infinitesimal part of the flow of time. For the living, birth is in the past and death is in the future. The present falls on the line somewhere between birth and death, depending on present age and length of life.

For the purpose of planning, present time is thought of as longer periods than the present instant. Assuming that the present is as much as a one-day segment of time, it is still but a dot (1 out of 25,550 days of a 70-year life) on the line of time somewhere between birth and death. Be cautioned, however, that that insignificant dot marking present time flows the full length of the continuum from birth to death. The way present time is spent has an influence upon both the length and quality of life.

In Voltaire's *Zadig; or, The Book of Fate*, the Grand Magus proposed to a group assembled in Babylon this question:

> "What is the longest and yet the shortest Thing in the World; the most swift and the most slow; the most divisible, and the most extended; the least valu'd, and the most regretted; And without which nothing can possibly be done: Which, in a Word, devours every Thing how minute soever, and yet gives Life and Spirit to every Object or Being however Great?"

Zadig pronounced it to be Time. His explanation was as follows:

> "Nothing," said he, "can be longer, since 'tis the Measure of Eternity; Nothing is shorter, since there is Time always wanting to accomplish what we aim at. Nothing passes so slowly as Time to him who is in Expectation; and nothing so swift as Time to him who is in the perfect Enjoyment of his Wishes. Its extent is to Infinity, in the Whole; and divisible to Infinity in part. All Men neglect it in the Passage; and all regret the loss of it when 'tis past. Nothing can possibly be done without it; it buries in Oblivion whatever is unworthy of being transmitted down to Posterity; and it renders all illustrious Actions immortal." The Assembly agreed unanimously that Zadig was in the right. ([1749] 1974, pp. 227–29)

With all its qualities, time is an inflexible resource that cannot be controlled. It cannot be produced, stored, recovered, changed, or managed in any way. It has to be used in some way the very instant it flows from future to present, but immediately, before it flows from present into the past. Some squander it, others spend it nonchalantly, and still others invest it in planned activities designed to meet carefully envisioned goals. While the individual is consuming time, time is consuming the individual. It gives, but it also takes away.

Measurements of Time

Since the very center of God's universe is order, the early measurements of time were done through observing the repetition of natural phenomena. A period of light followed by a period of dark became known as a day. A series of four phases of the moon was the rough measurement of a month, and the succession of four seasons, in temperate zones, was the essence of a year. The varying measurements of relatively long intervals of time used by agrarian societies are still in use as general reference points in marking time.

Mechanical devices for measuring time have an interesting history of invention and improvement. Sundials; dripping water; sand hourglasses; and burning candles, ropes, and lamps were means devised to divide the day into smaller segments. The clock did not come into being until the early fourteenth century. Early clocks had but one hand to separate the day into smaller but equal segments of time.

It was the industrial revolution and the urbanization of society that created a need to measure time even more accurately and synchronize it for the masses. Big Ben, the famous clock in the clock tower of the Houses of Parliament in London, calls attention to the importance of time during the middle 1800s. Big Ben was made large and located high in a tower so it could easily be seen and was fitted with bells so that it could be heard at a distance at the appointed times. As civilization advanced, man became more regimented by the timepieces he invented than by the cycles observed in nature.

The number and variety of mass-produced timepieces in use today attest to the fact that modern society is besieged and actually dominated by time-related activities and schedules at home, at work, and even during leisure time. Family members are regulated by alarm clocks designed to arouse them from rest, grandfather clocks that strike each quarter hour as a constant notice or warning, binary clocks that blink the seconds away as constant reminders of how fast time is fleeting, and clocks that control appliances to make them more efficient.

In addition to timepieces in the home, in the car, on exteriors of buildings, and in offices, almost everyone carries a personal timepiece. The wristwatch, a common personal timepiece, may have such special features as a second hand, stopwatch capability, or date and day readouts. It is often battery-powered or fully automatic and self-winding, to ensure an added degree of dependability. The sole purpose of the multiplicity of timepieces is to synchronize people with other people, schedules, and events. Timepieces are intended to keep people on time.

The common use of mechanical clocks and watches for measuring time by an industrial society in urban settings revolutionized the concept of time in several ways. Gurevich (1976) succinctly describes the changes:

> Possessing the means for measuring time precisely, and so of dividing it up into equal periods, men were bound, sooner or later, to become aware of the radical transformations the concept of time had undergone as a result of the evolution of society as a whole, and of the town in particular. Time for the first time, and for good, "extended" in a straight line, from the past to the future, passing through a point called the present. In earlier ages, the differences between past, present and future had been relative, and the dividing line between them movable; but with the triumph of linear time these differences became very precise, and present time was "compressed" until it was merely a point sliding continuously along the line which runs from past to future, transforming the future into the past. Present time became fleeting, irreversible and elusive. Man for the first time discovered that time, whose passing he had noted only in relation to events, did not cease even in the absence of events. As a result, an effort had to be made to save time, to use it rationally and to fill it with actions useful to man. (p. 242)

Science and technology have made it possible to measure time in smaller units and more accurately than would have been imagined only years before. The most accurate timekeepers today are atomic clocks that will not gain or lose a second in more than one hundred thousand years. As for slicing or segmenting time, the stopwatch does it down to fractions of a second. Computers are operated on nanosecond intervals (a nanosecond is one-billionth of a second). In 1982, newspapers commonly reported that Bell Laboratories had produced a flash of laser light that lasts thirty-millionth of a billionth of a second—only enough time to allow light to travel one-third the thickness of a human hair. The measurement, recorded in femtoseconds (one millionth of a billionth of a second), is the shortest interval of time yet recorded. At the opposite extreme, in probing the past, archaeologists using radioactive carbon clocks can measure with reasonable accuracy the age of objects that are tens of thousands of years old. While accurate measurements of time in minuscule amounts or at such distant times in the past may be critical to the scientist and researcher, they are but a figment of the imagination to the average person and have very little influence on daily living.

Worth of Time

Because time is a free resource, often it is not considered to have much value. However, it is time that the worker trades for salary and other rewards. For example, a teacher who earns a twenty thousand dollar salary with a four thousand dollar fringe benefit package by working 183 days a year trades each workday for $131.15. Absence from work because of illness, professional improvement activities, or some other legitimate reason makes the trade-off even more rewarding financially.

The purchase of an automobile is essentially the purchase of many workers' time. Significant amounts of workers' time are required to produce raw materials such as ore, petroleum, soybeans, and cotton; to manufacture iron, steel, plastics, and cloth; to convert these materials into parts and fixtures; to assemble the parts into an automobile; and to merchandize the finished product. People work for money; their time on the work force is only as valuable as the wages and salaries they are paid.

People are likely to value the things they spend time doing. The value is pegged to the amount of time spent on the project or activity. Teachers are more likely to value and use a curriculum if they have helped to create it. Involvement implies a commitment of time that, in turn, is expected to ripen into payoffs.

Countless numbers are not attuned to the value of time. They are not motivated to do much with it. In his book *The Games People Play* (1976), Berne presents as commonplace the somber picture in which "human life is mainly a process of filling in time until the arrival of death, or Santa Claus, with very little choice, if any, of what kind of business one is going to transact during the long wait" (p. 184). Those who are "filling in" time are waiting around for something to happen. Those who value time are making things happen.

A Consciousness of the Dimension of Time

The value of time was genuine to the unknown author who compared the use of time with the management of money:

> If you had a bank that credited your account each morning with $86,400 that carried over no balance from day to day and allowed you to keep no cash in your account and every evening cancelled whatever part of the amount you had failed to use during the day, what would you do?
> Draw out every cent, of course!
> Well, you have such a bank, and its name is "Time." Every morning it credits you with 86,400 seconds. Every night it rules off, as lost, whatever of this you have failed to invest to good purpose. It carries over no balances. It allows no overdrafts. Each day it opens a new account for you. Each night it burns the records of the day. If you fail to use the day's deposits, the loss is yours.
> There is no going back. There is no drawing against tomorrow. You must live in the present—on today's deposits. Invest it so as to get from it the utmost in health, happiness and success! (author unknown)

Asking for "a minute" can be a major encroachment on another person's time. The minute requested can stretch into a fifteen-minute or even greater loss of time to the one infringed upon. Those who use the time of another person, no matter how well, cannot give it back. The time-conscious person is fully aware that time that is given is gone. If given willingly, it is a gift; if not, it is a sacrifice. In either case, that part of life, be it a minute or an hour, is gone forever.

Sensitivity to Time

Sensitivity to time influences behavior. The child that has not developed to the point of understanding time engages in random activity in response to those stimuli that surface at the moment. The adult who is insensitive to time operates in much the same way. Earthly life appears aimless and at best is a mere state of existence.

Dru Scott, in the closing paragraph of her book *How to Put More Time in Your Life*, explains succinctly and with feeling the preciousness of time and advises on how to regard and use it. She writes:

> Time is a gift. It's always at your fingertips, always ready to be embraced and enjoyed. So greet this day with the eager delight you feel when someone who loves you places a gift in your hands.

Accept it joyfully. Appreciate its specialness. Treat it with care. Do your best with this day, and you will give yourself the gift of time. (p. 212)

Sensitivity to time can be assessed simply by observing what people say and do. The young cannot wait until they are old enough to drive a car, get a job, or do what they want to without parental approval or supervision. The old can hardly believe that another year has gone by so quickly or that the fiftieth wedding anniversary is only months away. Sensitivity to time changes with age.

Sensitivity to time or the lack of it also influences the way social and business transactions are done. Overnight "express" service is guaranteed, news of an event is expected "momentarily," and furniture is sold with assurance of "immediate delivery." We often hear people say things like "The doctor is running late," "The shipment did not arrive as expected," and "Don't go to that garage for automobile repairs if you don't want to waste a day."

Just how instant is "instant" soup? Language specifying a period of time or point in time can be exact, or it can be indefinite. The time-sensitive person will make the appointment at "5:00 P.M. sharp"; the time-insensitive one "will be over in a little while." The first appointment was specified in exact terms; the second was phrased in indefinite language.

The human body senses time through physical functions. Heartbeat and breathing measure time somewhat crudely. The body, a biological time clock, requires regular periods of sleep if it is to remain healthy. Body temperature, which climbs during the day and falls at night, may affect both mood and efficiency. Due to rhythmic functions of the body, individuals are likely to perform differently at different times of the day and at different times of the month.

The time-sensitive person knows about and takes advantage of these cyclic highs and lows at work and at play and schedules his or her activities with consideration of the body's built-in biorhythmic feedback. Some people may do better at desk work or mental activity early in the day and prefer physical tasks and exercise during the afternoon and evening. Others might perform better if the schedule were reversed. Knowing which schedule fits your physical makeup and then scheduling activities accordingly is a mark of the time-conscious person.

Reasoning about the dimension of time—or about any topic, for that matter—is a function only of the human mind, not necessarily of the whole person. The mind organizes and synthesizes knowledge into understandings. The intellectual resources for learning about the topic of time are many and varied. Almanacs, magazines, and newspapers offer adages, epigrams, maxims, and proverbs about time and its importance. Full-length books and research reports offer more comprehensive information. Time management seminars are tailor-made for executives, managers, supervisors, and other groups that express a need for this service. The attitudes, values, and feelings of participants are influenced by all these means. The full extent of the influence, however, is not realized until the affective qualities are internalized to the extent that they are expressed in habitual overt behavior. While much information on the improved use of time can be turned to for the purpose of changing behavior, few people make use of it and their minds remain unchallenged.

Thelen (1960) suggests that those sensitive to the dimension of time are able to link past events with visions of anticipated future events:

> The most fascinating question in the world is, How does one thing lead to another? Here we are, standing in the present but this is merely one tiny event in a long series that began with time and will end in the unforeseeable future. Time is a mountain whose peak is the present. The past slopes off one side and the future off the other. Looking in one direction we make explanations; looking in the other, predictions. People then, now, and in time to come will always be on the peak, midway between explanations and predictions; caught in both, both overlapping and each giving its unique flavor to the quest that is life. In looking backward we start with facts and then build an image; in looking forward we build an image and then, through action, make the facts. To the extent that we do both we are able to be wise. (p. 188)

Sensitivity to time is a trait that prompts one to review the past and forecast the future in arriving at credible answers to present-day problems. It provides the teacher with yet another mechanism with which to arrive at rational decisions and commonsense conclusions.

Uses of Time

The day is a unit commonly used for explaining how people spend their time. One fraternal organization suggests that the day be divided into three equal parts, with eight hours for work, eight hours for relaxation and recreation, and eight hours for sleep. The recipe does not take into consideration that weekends are spent somewhat differently than are weekdays. Perhaps the week is a more realistic unit than the day to employ in describing how people use their time.

Robinson (1977), in a social-psychological analysis of everyday behavior, found that "(1) sleep averaged remarkably close to the proverbial eight-hour-per-day figure, and (2) by the time all obligatory activities were taken into account, only about 20 percent of time remained free" (p. 186). From this information it is calculated that the average American's week of 168 hours is spent as follows: 78 hours involved in obligatory activities, 56 hours sleeping, and 34 hours of free time to use (see figure 1.3).

The obligatory activities in the Robinson research included work, housework, child care, meeting personal needs, and travel. Of the 78 hours for obligatory activities, 51 hours by employed men and 39 hours by employed women were spent working and commuting weekly. Free time was used for organizational activity, adult education, viewing and listening to mass media, socialization, and recreation. Age, affluence, educational level, employment status, and sex appeared to influence how free time was used.

Work time is given a value different from other time in that it is monitored externally for the purpose of maximizing output. The well-being of industry and ultimately of society is dependent upon how well workers use their time. Robinson (1977) found "that at least 12 percent of the time [that] individuals record as 'work' is spent

FIGURE 1.3. How Americans Use a Week

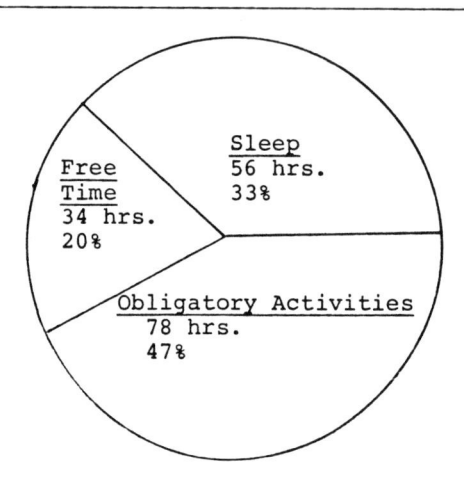

on non-work activities and personal business done at the workplace." He also found that "self-employed people put in a much longer than average workweek" (p. 182). The findings reveal that workers employed by others spend nearly five hours per forty-hour workweek not working, while the self-employed give additional hours to the job. Values of the two groups differ significantly.

The use and abuse of work time can be measured generally in terms of quality and quantity of production. The smallest component part, if unavailable or of inferior quality, can shut down a plant. The inexact formulation of a product can result in untold waste when it must be dumped. The recall of defective automobiles for exchange of parts and adjustments is a reflection on workmanship. The way work time is used can close a nuclear power plant, or it can produce an abundance of agricultural products. The use of time at the work place is heavily dependent on employee's attitudes about work. If attitudes are good, the fruits of labor also will be good and most rewarding.

Closing Statement

Time is an inflexible resource. It cannot be managed in any way. It must be used. How time is used can be managed. The ways time is invested have an influence on the kind of life that is lived.

Life is measured by time. Individuals consume time, and time consumes individuals. Time is free; it is a gift. To some it is a precious resource; to others it is something to be wasted.

Time can be used nonchalantly or invested thoughtfully. The ratio of the amounts of time given to sleep, play, and work is indicative of one's personal values. Achievements demonstrate purpose in life. To spend life and time effectively and efficiently is a need of most, but an accomplishment few master.

2
Managing Yourself

> If it is to be, it is up to me.
> —Author unknown

In the previous chapter it was stressed that time cannot be managed. Individuals must put themselves in control to take advantage of time as it flies by. Time is not the problem; the problem is managing *yourself* to use time. While you cannot control time, you can do something about how well you use time.

Managing yourself well in terms of using time can add years and excitement to your life. Using time in the best possible way to extend and enrich life is dependent to a great extent on "know-how" and self-discipline. It involves such exercises as making a thorough assessment of yourself, preparing a set of goals with priorities, adopting useful self-management tools, and making a commitment to use time to the fullest.

The way you spend time reveals much about you. When your activities are directed toward stated goals, when time scheduled for doing work is reasonably adequate, and when stress is unrelated to the resource of time, it is likely that you have discovered some of the secrets to managing yourself. Payoffs lead to refinements of self-management skills that, in turn, lead to greater payoffs.

Assessment of Self

Socrates admonished, "Know thyself." Knowing yourself is a prerequisite to managing yourself. Take time to reflect on what you say, what you do, and what you are. Be honest, objective, and thorough. A self-appraisal at any point in life can confirm your satisfaction with your life-style or initiate change in your behavior for the days and years ahead.

One kind of assessment may begin with an inventory of such background qualities as your education, training, experience, and talents, as well as of your values, attitudes, philosophy, and goals. What do you want out of life, and how realistic are your desires when related to your own strengths and weaknesses? Are you a time-oriented person? Are you an early-morning or late-night person? What is the state of your physical health? Have you attempted to match your personality with your energy cycle?

Kozoll, in a booklet on time management for educators, lists five distinct personality types and their characteristic time use behaviors (1982, p. 10). Kozoll's list is reproduced in figure 2.1. A review of the list in terms of your predominant mode of time use behavior will reflect your personality and how you tend to operate. In figure 2.1 put a check mark next to the time use behaviors that typify your style of operation. Kozoll notes that one cluster of traits tends to dominate in the personalities of individuals; by checking the items in the list that apply to you, you will be able to see where your time use behaviors "cluster" and which personality type you most closely resemble. By doing this assessment exercise, you may gain insights that will help you develop management strategies.

Another approach to self-assessment is value clarification. Lee and Pierce (1980) explain why value clarification is an important part of self-management:

> Before you can begin to consider HOW to get what you want, you must know WHY you want it. You have to stop and examine where your life is going today, where you'd like to be tomorrow, or next month, or next year. You should even consider exactly what you want to accomplish before you die.
>
> Determining your WHY's in life is really very simple. To accomplish it you will use a system called "Values Clarification." It's an easy way to decide what things in life have meaning and importance to you—what things you consider working for. (pp. 11-12)

Determine what things have meaning for you and are worth working for by doing the following exercises. Review your current resumé and then rewrite it as you would *like* it to be ten years from now. Also prepare a distinguished service citation that you would like

FIGURE 2.1. Time Use Personality Types Checklist

Goal-centered personalities

( ) Determine what needs to be done and how they wish to accomplish it
( ) Clearly assign priorities
( ) Regularly measure progress toward established goals
( ) Exclude activities that do not relate to those goals
( ) Are very comfortable because of clear target they wish to reach

Planning-oriented personalities

( ) Operate from a clear agenda or plan
( ) Organize and arrange activities for maximum effectiveness
( ) Exercise control over common interruptions
( ) Deal with the trivial or routine quickly or not at all
( ) Rarely procrastinate and always follow up to make sure what was planned is completed

Completing-focused personalities

( ) Define what is needed to finish assignments
( ) Organize work place to assure prompt completion
( ) Follow through on priorities with self and others
( ) Are very self-demanding and persistent

Emphasis-centered personalities

( ) Discriminate among priorities
( ) Establish and maintain a routine as much as possible
( ) Can say "no" to work and people as appropriate
( ) Calmly handle external demands
( ) Make decisions well under pressure

Limits-sensitive personalities

( ) Recognize personal energy and involvement limits and don't go beyond them
( ) Delegate assignments to others easily and well
( ) Can separate from work and job, leaving both at the end of the day
( ) Tend to be relaxed

Note: Adapted from C. E. Kozoll, Time Management for Educators (Bloomington, Ind.: Phi Delta Kappa Educational Foundation, 1982), p. 10. Copyright 1982 by Phi Delta Kappa Educational Foundation. Adapted by persmission.

to receive at some designated time in the future. After several weeks or possibly months, review the written exercises. Do you still have a strong desire to accomplish the things listed on the projected resumé and described in the distinguished service citation? If these goals continue to be important, set aside time to pursue them with vigor and persistence.

Keys to managing yourself are self-discipline and self-control. In terms of work habits, individual behavior ranges from that of the sluggard, who does not want to work, to that of the workaholic, who finds it hard to stop working. Most people find a reasonable balance between the two extremes.

Machlowitz (1980), in a study of workaholics, observed that "while workaholics do work hard, not all hard workers are workaholics." She uses the term "to describe those whose desire to work long is intrinsic and whose work habits almost always exceed the prescriptions of the job they do and the expectations of the people with whom or for whom they work. But the first characteristic is the real determinant. . . . It is in fact preferable to view workaholism as an approach or attitude toward working than as an amount of time at work" (pp. 12–13).

The word *sluggard* is often used to describe those persons who are habitually lazy and almost never achieve the prescription of the job they do and the expectations of the people with whom or for whom they work when inclined to work. Like workaholism, goldbricking or loafing can be viewed as an attitude toward work. Both extremes of behavior can be changed or modified to some extent. Presumably it is just as difficult to adjust the behavior of the workaholic as that of the sluggard. Of the two extremes in behavior, it is probable that more teachers are motivated to improve rather than worsen their utilization of time.

Goals, Objectives, Priorities

DETERMINING YOUR GOALS

How important are personal goals? A person without goals is living a life without purpose. Life without purpose is pointless, haphazard, and irrational. The goal-oriented, those who think through what it is that they want, have a remarkably better chance of getting it.

Webster's Seventh Collegiate Dictionary (1967) defines a goal as "the end toward which effort is directed." A goal is a target at which to shoot; it is the destination at the end of a journey. Goals may be perceived as terminal objectives. They are thought of generally in global terms and encompass such things as what you want to do, be, and have. They can be and often are unwritten but are more useful when written down and frequently reviewed.

Personal goals may be short-term, intermediate, or long-term and may relate to your private life or to family, profession, and community. They should be worth striving for, realistic, and obtainable. Goals provide direction for purposeful activities and authentic relationships. They add zest to living and pay off in increased productivity and rewarding achievements.

Figure 2.2 lists some examples of personal long-term goals that relate to private life, family, profession, and community. The categories are designed to help you consider the broader facets of life and living as you plan your use of time for the future. The categories can be eliminated, expanded, or changed to reflect your personal style of

FIGURE 2.2. Examples of Long-term Personal Goals

```
Private life
   Develop photography as hobby
   Be part-time director of local bank
   Write newspaper column on gardening
   Take extended cruise around world
Family
   Own and live on small farm
   Support offspring to prepare for profession of their
      choice
   Research family history
Profession
   Become public school chief administrative officer
   Win Fulbright Fellowship
   Write book on educational administration
   Establish national consulting agency
   Be active in National Association of Secondary School
      Principals
Community
   Become president of local service club
   Serve local church in highest layman's position
   Be elected to state legislature
   Be appointed trustee of college alma mater
```

organization. You will find that the categories for long-term goals apply equally well for determining intermediate and short-term goals.

Setting goals is a time for solitude, reflection, and even creative daydreaming. It is a serious business, in that life is being planned around the priceless resource of time. The output must have been formulated by you and for you. The goals you choose dictate the kinds of activity in which you become involved. Choose them carefully. Odiorne reminds us that "goal setting is a forward looking process, done by imperfect people in an imperfect world" (n.d., last page).

ENABLING OBJECTIVES

Enabling objectives help one to attain stated goals. They are conceptualized as steps or component parts that direct efforts toward the goal. Enabling objectives provide the detail necessary to reach the target or destination, while goals are the means for initiating plans in an uncomplicated way and providing a general direction. Enabling objectives, like the goals they support, should be clear, concise, realistic, worthwhile, and compatible.

To illustrate, here are some examples of enabling objectives that are supportive of the long-term goal "to become a public school chief administrative officer" (from figure 2.2):

1. Achieve tenure at the end of the first three years of teaching
2. Gain recognition as a master teacher from students, faculty, and administrators
3. Complete the Ed.M. degree program in educational administration with a 3.5 grade point average
4. Satisfy the requirements for a principal's certificate simultaneously with the completion of the Ed.M. degree
5. Become chairperson of the science department within eight years of appointment to the first teaching position
6. Seek committee assignments followed by elected positions in the teachers' association
7. Apply for principalship after serving three years as department chairperson
8. Obtain superintendent's certificate after achieving five years experience as a school administrator

Enabling objectives put into operation the tasks that culminate in general goals. Routine objectives are not exciting; the obvious ones do not need to be stressed. Few or many objectives can be written to help one accomplish a goal. To break them down too far is a waste of time, but not being meticulous enough can result in lack of direction.

PRIORITIES

A list of goals supported by enabling objectives is not an action instrument until both goals and objectives are given preferential ratings or rankings called priorities. Sequencing may depend upon such factors as experience, financial resources, scheduling, opportunity, or timeliness. The establishment of priorities brings order to the list. Prioritized goals and objectives make the list a working instrument, a tailor-made stratagem for using the time in your life in the way you want to use it.

A list of stratified goals and objectives is not intended to be a finished document but rather a changing, working document on which deletions, additions, and other kinds of changes can be made. The progressive realization of your objectives and goals indicates success. The list directs; the marked-up list redirects.

Lists of goals and objectives need revising on a regular basis. The short-term goals and objectives may be revised weekly or monthly; the intermediate ones quarterly or semi-annually; and the long-term ones at least annually. Revisions require reflection on the past and projection into the future. The process of goal setting can be expected to improve with experience.

Review the lists often. A daily review of the short-term objectives and a weekly survey of the others are not an uncommon practice among goal-oriented individuals. Keep the list on the dresser for morning review or on the nightstand next to the bed for evening scrutiny. Be intimately familiar with the list. Use it to apportion your time according to your goals in life.

Managerial Tools

Self-management techniques that have the potential of helping you achieve and excel in the things you do are referred to here as managerial tools. Managerial tools are tried and proven ways and means of accomplishing tasks that are often basic and repetitive in nature. Books and articles on how to do things in a systematic and exacting way have become more numerous in recent years. The research findings in the behavioral sciences that have been translated into layman's language in this literature are helping people overcome weaknesses, accomplish ambitions, avoid mistakes, and fulfill their aspirations in life more completely.

The basic tools recommended for self-management include but are not limited to (1) library resources, (2) a standard procedure for seeking the truth, (3) transactional analysis, (4) change strategy, and (5) the recording of time logs. Since it is expected that teachers have been introduced to most of these managerial tools, each is touched on here in only a cursory way as it relates to self-management.

LIBRARY RESOURCES

The pool of information available to help one manage oneself in this complex and ever-changing society is enormous. Libraries are excellent places to locate resources that can answer questions and solve problems; the information is there to assimilate. Yet, except for scholars, too few of us make adequate use of these resources and of mind-training activities.

Serif (1961) explains what the trained mind is and what it can do: "The trained mind, simply stated, is one which has been conditioned to deal effectively with the problems that arise. Characteristic of the trained mind is that it can recognize fact, that it can make a distinction, that it can draw an inference, that it can judge evidence, and that it can concentrate" (p. 80).

Library resources accommodate to individual needs. Knowledge and skills are learned in different ways and at different rates. Values and attitudes change as a result of reading and learning. Learning cannot be taken away from you. It is exhibited in your every action and behavior. Knowledge is power.

PROCEDURE FOR SEEKING TRUTH

The acts of thinking, problem solving, decision making, structuring of inquiry, and doing scientific research fit a general action model for seeking truth. The process described by the model has seven steps:

1. Select or recognize the problem.
2. Define the problem in clear, specific terms.
3. Develop tentative answers; construct hypotheses.
4. Get the facts; collect the data.
5. Classify the facts; analyze the data.

6. Arrive at a solution; draw conclusions.
7. Adopt solution, make decision, answer question, solve problem, or otherwise generalize results.

Beyer's model (1971) for structuring inquiry (figure 2.3), devised for teachers, covers the procedure in five steps supported by substeps. The steps provide the overview, while the substeps clarify and operationalize the procedures. Together they give structure to the processes of reasoning, problem solving, and decision making. Short cuts that result in inaccurate data or findings can be costly and a waste of time.

The procedures used to seek the truth are exacting, but they are not complicated. Steps cannot be reversed or skipped in the procedure. Each step is dependent upon the thoroughness of the work done on the preceding step or steps. The procedure discourages impulsive decisions. It engenders logical and rational thinking.

Seeking truth calls for true objectivity, which is probably the most difficult of all qualities to achieve when dealing with yourself. The Cooperative State Research Service (1965) gives an apt description of objectivity:

> Objectivity is actually an attitude of the mind. . . . [One] achieves it by schooling himself to view his findings and conclusions through the eyes of the wise critic. He achieves it by placing common-sense and reasoning ahead of bias and provincialism. He recognizes the power of imagination and creativity, yet the wisdom of restraint. He disciplines his mind to become responsive to innovation, quickened by divergent ideas. (inside front cover)

TRANSACTIONAL ANALYSIS

Transactional analysis is an intellectual tool that can provide insights into managing yourself by understanding the basics of behavior and feelings of other people. *Games People Play*, by Eric Berne (1976), and *I'm O.K., You're O.K.*, by Thomas A. Harris (1969), best-sellers, are recommended reading. Knowing the basics in transactional analysis can help you monitor whether your present use of time is constructive or wasteful. Awareness of the concept may urge you to get out of time-wasting situations or maneuver in such a way as to make them more productive.

Owens (1978), in his approach to time management, proposes the use of transactional analysis "as a framework . . . to promote consciously-chosen decisions about a person's use of his time." He lists the basic ways in which people use their time as (1) withdrawal,

FIGURE 2.3. The Process of Inquiring

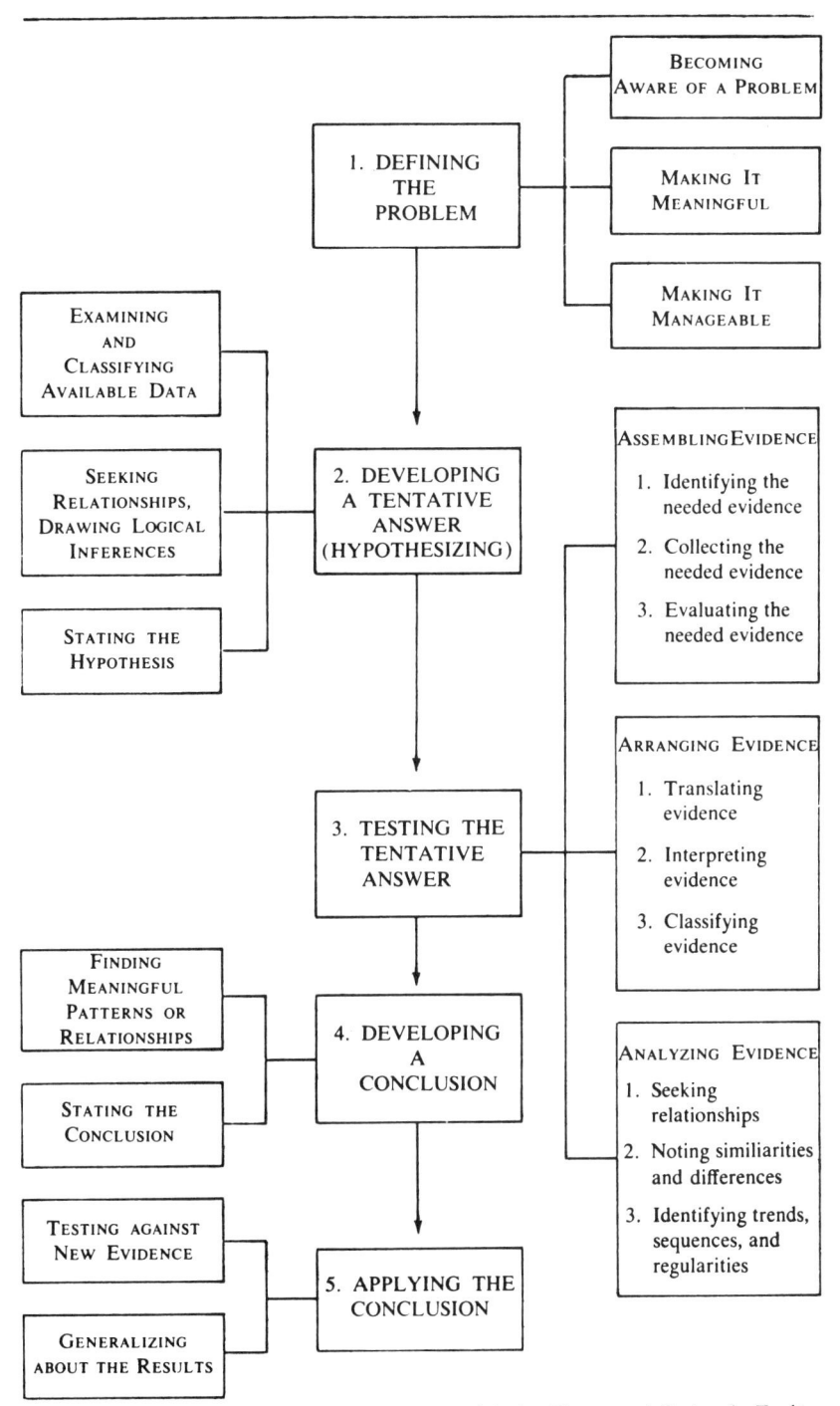

```
1. DEFINING THE PROBLEM
   ├── BECOMING AWARE OF A PROBLEM
   ├── MAKING IT MEANINGFUL
   └── MAKING IT MANAGEABLE

2. DEVELOPING A TENTATIVE ANSWER (HYPOTHESIZING)
   ├── EXAMINING AND CLASSIFYING AVAILABLE DATA
   ├── SEEKING RELATIONSHIPS, DRAWING LOGICAL INFERENCES
   └── STATING THE HYPOTHESIS

   ASSEMBLING EVIDENCE
     1. Identifying the needed evidence
     2. Collecting the needed evidence
     3. Evaluating the needed evidence

3. TESTING THE TENTATIVE ANSWER

   ARRANGING EVIDENCE
     1. Translating evidence
     2. Interpreting evidence
     3. Classifying evidence

   ANALYZING EVIDENCE
     1. Seeking relationships
     2. Noting similarities and differences
     3. Identifying trends, sequences, and regularities

4. DEVELOPING A CONCLUSION
   ├── FINDING MEANINGFUL PATTERNS OR RELATIONSHIPS
   └── STATING THE CONCLUSION

5. APPLYING THE CONCLUSION
   ├── TESTING AGAINST NEW EVIDENCE
   └── GENERALIZING ABOUT THE RESULTS
```

Note: From Barry K. Beyer, *Inquiry in the Social Studies Classroom: A Strategy for Teaching* (Columbus, Ohio: Charles E. Merrill, 1971), p. 50. Copyright © 1971 Charles E. Merrill Publishing Company, Columbus, Ohio. Reprinted by permission.

(2) rituals, (3) pastimes, (4) (life) "games," (5) activities (working, reading, studying, plowing, cooking, hobbies, sports), and (6) authentic (honest, sincere, and open) relationships. Owens writes that "the first four are generally a superficial waste of time (and life) and should be used by a healthy-minded person only occasionally and for brief periods. The last two are positive and constructive uses of time" (p. 2). He feels that "transactional analysis categories of the uses of time (rituals, pastimes, etc.) provide an ideal conceptual tool for *sensing fast* and consciously *electing* whether to use—or continue using—time at a given hour or day in a particular way" (p. 17).

CHANGE STRATEGY

Change, for purposes of this discussion, means to become different; to be transformed. Change in behavior implies the adoption of a new idea or practice. Adoption is an individual matter. Rogers (1962) defines adoption as "a decision to continue full use of an innovation" (p. 17).

Rogers, an Ohio State University researcher, lists five stages in the adoption process through which an individual passes from first hearing about an innovation to final adoption. The stages and type of behavior occurring at each stage are described as follows:

1. At the *awareness* stage, the individual is exposed to the innovation but lacks complete information about it.
2. At the *interest* stage, the individual becomes interested in the new idea and seeks additional information about it.
3. At the *evaluation* stage, the individual mentally applies the innovation to his or her present or anticipated future position and then decides whether or not to use it.
4. At the *trial* stage, the individual uses the innovation on a small scale to determine its utility in his or her own situation.
5. At the *adoption* stage, the individual decides to continue the full use of the innovation. (pp. 81-86)

Predispositions toward change differ among individuals. That is to say, not all individuals choose to adopt new ideas and practices at the same time. In change strategy literature, labels have been given to those with the various change orientations. The five types, according to the comparative length of time required to adopt, are (1) innovators, (2) early adopters, (3) early majority, (4) late majority, and (5) laggards. Innovators are the first to adopt, while laggards are the last. The distribution of individuals adopting a new idea over a period of time generally approximates a normal curve, with most of the adopters classified as early and late majority (Committee for the Study of the Diffusion of Farm Practices, 1962, pp. 1-12).

This study also presents selected characteristics of innovators and laggards, the two tails of the normal distribution curve. Innovators, when compared to laggards, are characterized as having a more favorable attitude toward science, placing less value on financial security, having more venturesome attitudes, reaching decisions more quickly, and taking risks. Innovators as a group have more formal education, a higher level of intelligence, and a greater ability to deal with abstractions than laggards as a group. Innovators are more active in formal organizations, more cosmopolitan, have a higher social status, greater prestige, and higher incomes than laggards. Laggards as a group place more trust in traditional beliefs, depend more on personal contacts for information, and, as a group, are older than innovators. They have fewer contacts with sources of new ideas, stronger ties with family, and lower social status than innovators (pp. 3-6).

The study also noted that "an innovator for one practice is likely to be an innovator for another practice" (p. 5). It is expected that a laggard for one practice is likely to be a laggard for another practice. If so, it appears that each individual's adoption behavior is likely to be consistent.

You can use your knowledge of the characteristics of innovators and laggards as a yardstick for assessing your own adoption behavior. Are you willing to change? Do you resist change? Or are you somewhere in the middle? Knowing about the adoption process and being able to assess your own disposition toward change are assets for planning a self-management program.

HABIT CONTROL

According to *Webster's Seventh Collegiate Dictionary* (1967), a habit is "an acquired mode of behavior that has become nearly or completely involuntary." There are at least two hidden dangers in dealing with habit: (1) since a habit is subconscious and automatic, it is difficult to control; and (2) it may be a negative or an undesirable behavior. McCay (1959) cautions, "Any moment you are preoccupied, acting habitually, it is a moment you are not free to manage your time" (p. 33). The riddle "Your Servant, or Master," in figure 2.4, offers further insight about habit control.

Habitual behavior uses much of our time. An assessment of habitual behavior is a part of managing yourself. How much of your time is spent in behavior that is automatic and unmanaged? How

FIGURE 2.4. Your Servant or Master

I am your constant companion. I am your greatest helper or your heaviest hindrance.

I will push you surely forward to success, or I will drag you down to failure. It is as you will.

I am completely at your command. Half of the tasks that you do, you might just as well turn over to me and I will do them quickly, correctly and without bother. Yes, or I will leave them undone, and let them hang on your neck like a curse. IT IS AS YOU WILL.

I am not easily managed. You need merely be firm with me. Show me JUST EXACTLY HOW YOU WANT THINGS DONE and, after a few lessons, I will do them automatically.

IF YOU DON'T SHOW ME, I SHALL NEVER LEARN, AND THE MORE YOU GIVE ME TO DO, THE QUICKER THE WRECK WILL COME. You see, I have no sense of pride. I know myself and I am square with you.

I am the trusted servant of all successful men. Yes, and alas, equally the servant of all failures. Those who are successful, I made successful. Those who are failures, I made failures. That was not my fault. It was theirs. I build or destroy. It is all one to me.

I am not a machine. But I work with all the precision of a machine, plus all the intelligence of a man. You may run me for profit or run me for ruin. It makes no difference to me.

Take me, train me, be firm with me, keep me in the right direction, use me, and I will put THE WORLD AT YOUR FEET. Be easy with me and I will destroy you.

Who am I? I AM HABIT.

Note: From *Be Somebody--Do Something Useful, Grow the Best That's in You* (Chicago: International Harvester Co., 1941), p. 72. Reprinted with permission.

---

much habitual behavior is serving you well and is worth keeping? How do you cast aside habits that waste time or are otherwise undesirable?

Managing yourself requires getting rid of undesirable habits and adopting new ones. Fensterheim and Baer (1975), in a book awarded honorable mention by the National Media of the American Psychological Association, list five steps to ensure change in habits:

1. Identify the habit you want to change.
2. Make a contract of intention that you want to change your behavior.
3. Examine the situation to see if you can make the unwanted act harder to perform and the desired act easier to perform.
4. Discover what consequences of your unwanted behavior serve to reinforce it. You must search out the immediate consequences of the act.
5. Establish the desired act. (pp. 186-99)

Mackenzie and Waldo (1981), in a book on time management tailored to meet the needs of today's woman, recognize that self-management involves the breaking of bad work habits and developing new ones. They offer six steps for developing good management habits for using time:

1. *Recognize the difficulty.* Longtime bad habits aren't broken easily.
2. *Develop a better way.* The best defense is a good offense. The easiest way to break a bad habit is to replace it.
3. *Launch the new habit strongly.* Weak initiatives die quickly.
4. *Go public.* By announcing it, you become committed.
5. *Repeat it often.* Take every opportunity to practice and reinforce it.
6. *Allow no exceptions.* Exceptions quickly become the rule, and you'll be back in your old bad habits. (pp. 23-24)

Everyone has a set of values. In governing yourself, you know which are good and which are bad habits. Essentially, habits help you to use time well or poorly in attaining established goals. Immediate attention to prioritized tasks, full concentration on the project at hand, and meeting predetermined deadlines are thought of as good habits. Socializing before getting down to work, daydreaming on the job, and being habitually late are regarded as less desirable behavior.

To change behavior is not easy. Sorting out good and bad habits is a beginning. A plan to eliminate the bad and adopt the good is a logical next step. The secret of success, however, is in implementing the plan and sticking to it until the good habit replaces the bad one. A successful first experience tends to make the experiences that follow less arduous. In other words, success begets success.

TIME LOGS

The time log is a managerial tool for assessing how you use your time. When your effectiveness seems to be slipping or when you begin to question where the day went, time log data are useful in diagnosing how you use your time. Some possible symptoms of poor time use by a teacher are detailed in figure 2.5.

Everyone knows in a general way how he or she has spent the day—in sleep, at work, and with free time. When one tries to remember exactly how the work time and free time were spent, though, the kinds of activities and amount of time spent at each become more difficult to determine. One way to find out how you are really spending your time is to record everything you do for a week on a time calendar. Figure 2.6 is an example of a completed daily time log for a teacher.

Even the one-day log reported in figure 2.6 is revealing. It shows that Mr. Crawford allowed himself seven hours of sleep, used about four hours for personal and family activities, invested more than three hours in professional improvement and public relations, logged one hour of travel time to and from school, and spent nine hours teaching and doing related work at school and at home. An analysis of the log might cause Mr. Crawford to question whether the hour of travel time could be shortened or used to better advantage. Should he have said no to the request to speak at the Lions Club meeting, or

FIGURE 2.5. Possible Symptoms of Poor Time Use by a Teacher

Often reports late to school
Often uses vacation days and weekends just to catch up
Has unread professional journals piled high in office
Feels he or she is only one who can do a job right
Has little or no time available for planning
Stays in school long after closing time
Uses obsolete visual aids and handouts for class
Often absent from professional and in-service meetings, seminars, and conferences
Carries oversized briefcases filled to capacity
Has student appointments stacked up
Has disorganized desk and storage areas
Has broken or inoperable audiovisual or laboratory equipment
Lets school work dominate life at home
Is slow at returning phone calls
Uses outdated courses of study and lesson plans
Is behind in reports, grades, and record keeping
Shows effects of stress visibly

FIGURE 2.6. Sample Daily Time Log

Name	Wayne Crawford. Date January 6

Time (a.m.)	Activity
6:00	Awoke, exercised, showered, and dressed for school
6:30	Had breakfast
6:45	Developed list of things to do today
7:00	Commuted to school
	Listened to news on car radio
7:30	Checked in at office
	Visited with other faculty
	Borrowed 16-mm. projector for class
7:45	Met student with problem at classroom door
	Prepared physics laboratory exercise
	Read morning announcements
8:00	Taught physics I class
8:45	Supervised physics I laboratory
9:30	Taught physics II class
10:15	Supervised physics II laboratory
	Sent disciplinary case to office
11:00	Had lunch
	Checked on disciplinary case in office
11:30	Taught chemistry I class

Time (p.m.)	
12:15	Taught chemistry II class
1:00	Had conference period and (1) updated plan book; (2) updated student records; (3) mimeographed copies of two handouts
2:00	End of school classes
	Held meeting with photography club
3:00	Returned 16-mm. projector
	Placed three telephone calls to parents of students
3:30	Worked on physics examination
4:00	Commuted to home
	Stopped at bank to get check cashed
	Stopped at store to get milk and bread
4:30	Had coffee and read evening newspaper
	Repaired leaking faucet in kitchen
	Enjoyed the family
6:15	Made presentation at Lions Club Dinner Meeting
8:30	Prepared assignment for university in-service class
10:00	Watched television
	Prepared announcement for school newsletter
	Wrote letter of recommendation for graduate
11:00	Went to bed

was it a worthwhile investment of time? Could he have used any portion of the day to better advantage? What will the seven-day log reveal? Are his activities moving him toward the attainment of established goals? If not, what changes in his use of time might be profitable?

Now that you have reviewed Mr. Crawford's one-day time log, what about you? How is your time being spent? Test yourself. Prior to keeping an actual time log, make a list of the activities in your weekly routine and estimate the amount of time given to each. Next, keep a log of activities for one week and record the time used doing each. Compare the estimated with the actual data.

It is likely that you are spending time in ways and amounts that will surprise you. Some unexpected conclusions that other educators have drawn from time log data are:

- Memory does not afford a very reliable record.
- Much time is spent on routine tasks and activities with low priorities.
- Little time is invested in planning and working toward established goals.
- School-directed activities take precedence in appointment calendars.
- Uncommitted time during the school day is limited to about one hour
- Time is wasted in roughly the same way each day and each week.

An analysis of how you use your time can be enlightening, amazing, or both. You can blame the results in the actual log on an abnormal week, or you can accept them as a closer approximation to the truth than the data recalled from memory. Time logs provide the actual data for answering questions, providing insights, and stimulating change in time use behavior.

Making a Commitment

Commitments shape and consume life—that gift that we often do not appreciate or understand. The riddle that follows describes the life we exchange for commitments that we make without regard to their worth.

"What is the Thing we receive, without being ever thankful for it; which we enjoy, without knowing how we came by it; which we give away to others, without knowing where 'tis to be found; and which we lose, without being any ways conscious of our Misfortune?" . . . Zadig . . . concluded it was *Life*. (Voltaire, [1749] 1974, p. 230)

Managing yourself is managing your life; managing your life is managing your time. It is putting yourself in control; doing more of what you want to do; and being more conscious of your subconscious behavior. Ultimately your life and success are affected by the way or the level at which you manage yourself. Your obligation goes even further than to yourself. If you are a teacher, you must have a greater capacity to manage yourself, because you are an example with profound influence on younger lives in the process of formation—your students.

The rewards of being organized are self-evident. The organized person accomplishes more, does things well, is decisive, proceeds with confidence, meets deadlines, checks progress toward goals, and uses time well. A self-management program yields benefits that in turn nurture the self-management program. The cycle has a tendency to intensify as one phase initiates another.

Closing Statement

Being able to manage yourself to your own satisfaction is one of the greatest of achievements. The recipe includes knowing yourself; charting the directions for investing your time; and mastering the knowledge, skills, and attitudes to help you succeed.

Step back and take a look at yourself. Be as objective as is possible. Find out who you are, what you enjoy doing, and how you act and react. Try to understand yourself.

Give purpose to life. Estimate your present station in life and project what you want out of life at predetermined points along the way. Establish realistic goals that target your ambitions.

Latch on to tried and proven ways of doing things. Be aware of and use self-management aids that guard against pitfalls. Rely on experience, as necessary, to accommodate to self and adjust to the broad spectrum of change that is inevitable.

Put yourself in control. Summon the energy and apply self-discipline to attain the life-style and the positions in life that you seek. These are the ultimate rewards for managing yourself well.

3
Institutional Time Constraints and Bonuses

> Observe a method in the distribution of your time. Every hour will then know its proper employment, and no time will be lost.
> —Bishop Horne

The teacher manages instructional activities within an institutional framework that regulates and governs the professional's "in-school" time, measured in minutes. Most of the teacher's in-school time is scheduled by others. Laws, policies, handbooks, calendars, schedules, and memoranda govern the teacher while in school much as a magnetic tape controls the modern lathe or a computer program directs a robot in a factory.

Bartholomew and Gardner (1982) have documented the use of time by the American schoolteacher. They report that "the mean number of teaching days for all teachers in the 1980–81 school year was 180. The mean number of days scheduled for all teachers in the 1980–81 school year for activities other than teaching (such as orientation and in-service) was 6" (p. 59). The contract year for teachers averages 186 days.

A major part of the teacher's time is spent teaching, in school. Time is also spent on school duties other than teaching, both in and out of school. Bartholomew and Gardner describe the weekly work load:

The average school workweek for all teachers was . . . 36.5 hours.
In 1981, the average number of hours spent weekly after the required workday on *instruction-related activities* such as lesson preparation and paper grading was 7.5 hours for all teachers.
An average of 1.7 hours was spent weekly by all teachers in 1981 on *noncompensated, noninstructional* activities such as bus duty or club advising.
In 1981, the mean number of hours that all teachers spent weekly on *all teaching duties* was 45.9. (pp. 51-60)

Teachers' workdays and work years have in them a generous amount of unencumbered time. Assuming (1) a professional workday with two hours for teacher-directed activities, and (2) 60 nonteaching days per year—excluding 186 school days, 104 weekend days, and 10 vacation days—a teacher has 852 hours, or more than 106 eight-hour days, of unstructured time per year to schedule for the purpose of meeting goals (table 3.1). Deciding how much of the time is used for professional pursuits and how well it is used is the prerogative of the teacher.

An awareness of both structured and unencumbered professional time is critical to the well-being of the teacher, the school district, and students. The teacher's day is longer than the school day; the teacher's year is longer than the school year. Professional activity beyond the school day and school year is more flexible than the in-school regimen. Since the teacher has a reasonable amount of control over some portions of the professional day and part of the calendar year, investing this unencumbered time should be most exciting and rewarding.

School Law

Public school education is the responsibility of individual states. State statutes to a considerable extent fix the rights and duties of public school teachers, who are generally licensed. As such they are directed and protected by statutes, court decisions, and administrative law. Some of these directives focus on teachers' time.

Public school law designates when teachers are expected to work and when they are not required to work. The requirements differ from state to state. One state may mandate the length of the school year at 175 days, while another may set it at 185 days. There are statutes on certification, tenure, dismissal, and retirement. Each has a bearing on how teachers use their time and their lives.

TABLE 3.1. Professional Time Inventory (One-year Analysis)

Other-structured Time (during Teaching Day)	Hours per Day	Days per Year	Hours per Year
Teaching classes; study hall assignments; activity and assembly periods; other instructional duties	6	180	1,080

Teacher-directed Time	Hours per Day	Days per Year	Hours per Year
During teaching day: includes both instruction-related and noncompensated, non-instructional activities such as preparing classes, cocurricular activities, reading student papers, doing reports, attending meetings, self-improvement meetings	2	186	372
During noncontract part of year:[a] professional improvement, involvement in professional associations, writing, educational travel, research	8	60	480
Total teacher-directed time per year			852

a. Excludes the 186 days of school, the 104 weekend days, and 10 vacation days. Remaining are 60 8-hour days.

The list of public holidays designated by state statute usually includes

- New Year's Day
- Martin Luther King's Birthday
- Lincoln's Birthday
- Washington's Birthday
- Good Friday
- Memorial Day
- Independence Day
- Labor Day
- Columbus Day
- Armistice or Veterans' Day
- Thanksgiving Day
- Christmas

Additional public holidays that may be observed are statehood days, days of religious observance, and any other days designated by the governor of the state or the president of the United States.

New Jersey law, for example, states that

> no teaching staff member shall be required to perform his duties on any day declared by law to be a public holiday and no deduction shall be made from such member's salary by reason of the fact that such a public holiday happens to be a school day and any term of any contract made with any such member which is in violation of this section shall be void. (N.J.S.A. 18A:25-3, p. 18)

Local Board of Education Policy

The local board of education enforces school law promulgated by the state. It also establishes policies under which its schools operate. Public school teachers are employees of school districts and their boards of education. In addition to state laws, public school teachers are subject to reasonable rules and regulations enacted by their board of education. Personnel policies issued by the board of education cover such areas as terms and tenure of employment, promotion, dismissal, and salaries. Personnel rules and regulations negotiated between the board of education and the teachers' association or union supposedly result in reasonable terms. The process gives teachers a voice in determining, within the law, how their professional time is to be spent.

Boards of education typically make the following decisions relating to the use of teachers' time:

- Determine the dates between which schools of the district shall be open in accordance with the law
- Are involved in collective bargaining or otherwise tender teacher employment contracts
- Inform teachers, upon employment, of the duties and obligations that are conditions of employment
- Grant permission to teachers to attend professional improvement meetings, take leaves of absence, etc.

Boards of education purchase costly professional time from teachers, and they stipulate to some extent in writing when and how they want that time to be used. They also set the terms for benefits and compensations.

The Teaching Contract

A teaching contract is a personal service agreement between the board of education and the teacher. Teacher employment contracts are prepared by the board of education. Their provisions (fairly standard across all the states) are described by Martinez, Zaino, Weger, and Collins in their book *Basic School Law*. According to Martinez et al., "Teacher employment contracts must specify: (a) the date the employment is to begin, (b) the kind of certificate held by the teacher and its expiration date, (c) the salary to be paid, and (d) such other matters as may be necessary to a full and complete understanding" (1978, p. 116). Parts a, b, and c are necessarily explicit. Part d is general but is usually supported by a set of specific directives that must definitely be taken into account when one is assessing the investment of time that the teacher is expected to make. In the contract packet should be a copy of the agreement between the board of education and the education association or union and of terms and conditions of employment, if arrived at through collective bargaining. Other helpful directives likely to be in the contract packet are a job description, school philosophy statement, faculty handbook, and school-year calendar.

A class schedule, plan book, extracurricular assignments, report forms, and a constant stream of administrative memoranda follow. All have a direct bearing on the way in which teacher's time will be invested and distributed to meet the terms and conditions of the contract.

Job Description for Teacher

Job descriptions follow job analyses. According to the U.S. Department of Labor, a job analysis entails "the identification of the tasks which comprise the job and of the skills, knowledges, abilities, and responsibilities that are required of the worker for successful performance and that differentiate the job from others." The Department of Labor provides an overview of the job analysis process:

> Basically, there are but three parts to the analysis of any job: (1) The job must be identified completely and accurately; (2) the tasks of the job must be described completely and accurately; (3) the requirements the job makes upon the worker for successful performance must be indicated. . . . The categories of information that must be obtained and reported in order to meet the requirements for a complete analysis of a job are four in number and have been formalized into a measurement device that is designated as the "Job Analysis Formula." These four categories are: "What the worker does," "How he does it," "Why he does it," and "The skill involved in doing it." (1966, p. 3)

The National School Boards Association (1982) views a job description as "the blueprint or guide for work to be accomplished" (p. 38). The job description is a vehicle used to delegate those activities for which the teacher is to be held accountable. Rutherford (1978) cautions that job description should not be confused with job responsibility. He explains:

> A job description simply tells you what you are not allowed not to do. It tells you the things that you must do, but it doesn't spell out some of the most important things you are being paid to do. It doesn't say when, where, how and what to take the initiative on. . . . It doesn't outline the extra steps that make the difference. It may tell you about doing a passable job but it doesn't tell you much of anything about doing the best job. (p. 80)

The *Dictionary of Occupational Titles* (U.S. Department of Labor, 1977) is a recognized source of standardized descriptions of job titles. It has differentiated job descriptions for teachers employed in primary, elementary, and secondary schools; junior colleges; and universities. The job description for secondary school teacher (no. 091: 227-101) is as follows:

> Teaches one or more subjects, such as English, mathematics, or social studies, to students in public or private secondary schools: Instructs students in subject matter, utilizing various teaching methods, such as lecture and demonstration, and uses audiovisual aids and other materials to supplement presentations. Prepares teaching outline for course of study, assigns lessons, and corrects homework papers. Administers tests to evaluate pupils' progress, records results, and issues reports to inform parents of progress. Keeps attendance records. Maintains discipline in classroom and school yard, participates in faculty and professional meetings, educational conferences, and teacher training workshops. Performs related duties, such as sponsoring one or more special activities of student organizations, assisting pupils in selecting course of study, and counseling them in adjustment and academic problems. May be identified according to subject matter taught. (p. 67)

Job descriptions are written in many styles and with the use of a wide variety of resources. The National School Boards Association (1982) lists eight characteristics of an effective job description in education. A job description should

> Specify the job's title
> Indicate the kind and extent of skills, knowledge, and abilities required by the job
> Make clear the job's position in the chain of supervision
> Relate the job to its ultimate client—the student—and to the objectives of the educational program
> Outline the major performance responsibilities that make up the job's content
> State the terms of employment and make reference to evaluative criteria for the job
> State how often the incumbent's performance will be evaluated according to the description's evaluative criteria
> Provide for the incumbent's acknowledgement of the details of his job description (p. 38)

A job description is an administrative document. It is a vehicle for delegating responsibility to the teacher for the delivery of instruction. In it the role of the teacher is defined in such a way that the administrator and the teacher have a common understanding of the teacher's job and expectations about performance. The job description aids the administrator in directing the use of a teacher's time, gives the teacher a sense of understanding about the job, and, hopefully, through these benefits, improves the students' level of achievement in the school.

A model job description for a teacher, prepared by the National School Boards Association, is shown in figure 3.1. While it does not necessarily reflect official National School Boards Association policy, this job description can be edited as necessary to meet local school requirements. It describes how the teacher's time is to be used in terms of performance responsibilities and in terms of employment.

School Calendars

School calendars stipulate opening and closing dates of the school year and also designate holidays and vacation periods. In addition, they may list other dates, such as those for parent-teacher conferences and open houses. Teachers and students need the calendars for planning academic programs and scheduling out-of-school activities.

The school calendar influences both the professional and personal lives of teachers. When school closes near the end of June, inservice courses in colleges and universities may already be in session, which eliminates that professional improvement option. A school calendar that is longer than the state-mandated school year infringes on teachers' personal time by one or more days. When teachers have the opportunity to offer input into the structuring of the school calendar, they would be unwise not to exercise this right.

The school calendar reveals a bonus of time for teachers that other professionals rarely experience. The school year ranges in length from 155 to 190 days, with the mode being 180 days. The calendar is liberally peppered with holidays, more so in urban than rural areas. The summer vacation can vary from a bit more than two months to nearly three months.

Holidays and summer vacation add up to some 60 days, excluding all 2-day weekends. The 60 days outside the school year, plus some of the weekend days, offer the teacher a wealth of time in a variety of packages. Holidays and vacation days for schoolchildren can be rationalized as holidays and vacation days by teachers. Teachers can also justify using some of that time in a second job for additional income. Still others will invest this gift of time in advanced degrees, teacher conferences and workshops, related reading, and other professional activities.

FIGURE 3.1 Model Job Description

TITLE: Teacher

QUALIFICATIONS:
1. [Certificate, license, or other legal credential required.]
2. [Degree(s) required and area of major study.]
3. [Kind and amount of prior job experience required.]
4. Such alternatives to the above qualifications as the Board may find appropriate and acceptable.

REPORTS TO: [Person designated by the Board or the superintendent.]

SUPERVISES: [Staff members designated by the Board or the superintendent.]

JOB GOAL: To help students learn subject matter and skills that will contribute to their development as mature, able, and responsible men and women.

PERFORMANCE RESPONSIBILITIES:
1. Meets and instructs assigned classes in the locations and at the times designated.
2. Plans a program of study that, as much as possible, meets the individual needs, interests, and abilities of the students.
3. Creates a classroom environment that is conducive to learning and appropriate to the maturity and interests of the students.
4. Prepares for classes assigned, and shows written evidence of preparation upon request of immediate superior.
5. Encourages students to set and maintain standards of classroom behavior.
6. Guides the learning process toward the achievement of curriculum goals and--in harmony with the goals --establishes clear objectives for all lessons, units, projects and the like to communicate these objectives to students.
7. Employs a variety of instructional techniques and instructional media, consistent with the physical limitations of the location provided and the needs and capabilities of the individuals or student groups involved.
8. Strives to implement by instruction and action the district's philosophy of education and instructional goals and objectives.
9. Assesses the accomplishments of students on a regular basis and provides progress reports as required.
10. Diagnoses the learning disabilities of students on a regular basis, seeking the assistance of district specialists as required.

FIGURE 3.1 (continued)

---

11. Takes all necessary and reasonable precautions to protect students, equipment, materials, and facilities.
12. Maintains accurate, complete, and correct records as required by law, district policy, and administrative regulation.
13. Assists the administration in implementing all policies and rules governing student life and conduct, and, for the classroom, develops reasonable rules of classroom behavior and procedure, and maintains order in the classroom in a fair and just manner.
14. Makes provisions for being available to students and parents for education-related purposes outside the instructional day when required or requested to do so under reasonable terms.
15. Plans and supervises purposeful assignments for teacher aide(s) and volunteer(s) and, cooperatively with department heads, evaluates their job performance.
16. Strives to maintain and improve professional competence.
17. Attends staff meetings and serves on staff committees as required.

TERMS OF EMPLOYMENT: Ten, eleven, or twelve month year. Salary and work year to be established by the Board.

EVALUATION: Performance of this job will be evaluated in accordance with provisions of the Board's policy on Evaluation of Professional Personnel.

Approved by: _____ Date: _____

Reviewed and agreed to by: _____ Date: _____
                           (Incumbent)

Note: From National School Boards Association, School Personnel Management System (Locator 3.25) (Washington, D.C.: NSBA, 1982). Copyright 1982 by National School Boards Association. Reprinted by permission.

Personal needs, values, and other influences direct teachers in their use of holiday and vacation time. The desire for tenure motivates beginning teachers to engage in professional improvement activities. Tenured teachers may prepare for administrative and college teaching positions, or their goal may be to become and remain outstanding classroom teachers. Dedication to the profession and the ability to manage oneself are significant influences on how teachers use their holiday and vacation time.

Daily Schedule, Class Schedule

The daily schedule includes more than just the class schedule. It accounts for time teachers are scheduled for both before and after class. Teachers are expected to be in school a designated length of time before classes begin and after they end. This requirement is understandable; it is the amount of time that must be spent before and after classes that is controversial. Just 15 minutes in the classroom before and after classes each day during an 180-day school year adds up to 5,400 minutes—90 hours—or more than 11 days of 8 hours each.

In some districts teachers are required to "clock in and clock out" by hours and minutes. In others a "sign in and sign out" roster is used to notify superiors of teacher arrival and departure. Arrival and departure information is a managerial necessity, but the method used to record it is often an issue between administrators and teachers.

And finally, teachers are requested and expected to report to school earlier than normal and stay later than usual on occasion without additional compensation. How early, how late, and how often are matters of reasonableness that may be perceived differently by administrators than by teachers. Time is lost in minutes that accumulate into hours and days. Petty demands for additional time spent in school are serious encroachments on teacher nonteaching time. They can strain administrator-teacher relationships.

Teaching schedules are a means of informing teachers where they are to be each period of the school day and what they are to be doing. For example, a schedule could assign Teacher X to the industrial arts shop to teach woodworking II during the second period. Schedules also note homeroom assignments and such nonteaching activities as planning or conference periods, cafeteria duty, study halls, and lunch.

Teaching schedules provide experienced teachers with clues about time demands. They realize, for example, that

- The more courses or subjects they are scheduled to teach, the more preparation they must do

- A period of cafeteria duty or study hall duty in the schedule requires no preparation time
- Homeroom, shop, and laboratory responsibilities consume time over and above that scheduled
- Section 11A is a small class and therefore easier to teach than section 11D, which is large
- Room 112 is more difficult than room 218 to prepare for audiovisual presentations
- A preparation period is a bonus in a schedule

Teachers know that fair and equitable teaching schedules and work loads require a full measure of evenhandedness, taking account of teachers' assignment preferences and their known capabilities and qualifications.

A daily planning or conference period is to be regarded as a work period. If used productively, it can result in fewer items in the briefcase by the end of the school day and less homework for the teacher. It can profitably be used for such duties as

- Preparing and updating lesson plans
- Reading and grading student papers
- Developing and preparing audiovisual presentations
- Returning telephone calls
- Maintaining the classroom, laboratory, or shop equipment
- Answering administrative directives
- Completing reports
- Holding student/parent conferences
- Reading professional journals and technical materials
- Working on public relations activities

When working in school, priority should be given to duties that require for their completion the use of school resources such as data banks, files, reference books, and special equipment.

One-half of a workday can be gained in a week by using each daily planning or conference period in a constructive way. An alternative to working is to spend the period in the teachers' lounge socializing or just relaxing. Either practice can develop into a daily routine called habit, and either can easily be rationalized by the teacher. The payoffs to the teacher differ, as do the impressions made on superiors. Observations would suggest that teachers who waste planning and conference time are more frequently assigned emergency duties during those periods than are the busy teachers.

Nonteaching Duties and Professional or Community Involvement

Teachers' primary responsibility is to teach, and they prefer it to be that way. According to one survey,

> When asked how they would choose to spend additional work time, Dade County teachers overwhelmingly selected activities related to classroom rather than schoolwide matters. Ninety-one percent of the respondents chose teacher related activities. . . . Their press is toward effort where psychic rewards occur—in work directly connected with their students. As an indication of preference for classroom versus schoolwide activities, the responses are unambiguous; the vast majority of respondents—5,448 out of 5,991—chose to spend additional time on classroom tasks rather than working with the school at large. (Lortie, 1975, p. 164)

Teachers voice concern about the increasing nonteaching load imposed upon them. In the past, little attention was paid to nonteaching duties in contracts. Often teachers were unaware of how much time they were required to give to extracurricular activities and how to respond to invitations and assignments to assume any of a myriad of nonteaching responsibilities. With the advent of agreements, the nonteaching duties of the teacher are being clarified.

A review of the literature reveals that nonteaching duties can be stratified into three categories: those that can be assigned to teachers; those that teachers cannot be compelled to do; and those that are not clearly defined. Generally teachers *can* be assigned to supervise study halls and school-sponsored events, and they *can* be required to attend open houses and teachers' workshops; but they *cannot* be compelled to perform such duties as custodial service, traffic duty, inventorying and storing books, and school bus driving; and they *may or may not* be assigned to extracurricular duties, depending on conditions of reasonableness. Such conditions of reasonableness that are helpful in assessing assignments or considering extracurricular activities include

- The relationship of the duty to teaching
- The relationship of the duty to the teacher's academic field

- Whether the duty is to be performed outside the school day
- Whether duties are distributed evenly and without discrimination among all teachers
- Whether assignments are being compounded to the extent of being onerous and time-consuming

If nonteaching assignments become a burden, the onus is on the teacher to prove abuse.

Teachers may volunteer to perform nonteaching duties with or without pay or released time. In addition to contributing to professional objectives of the teacher, such extracurricular activities as intramural sports, clubs, school newspapers, student council, wrestling, and yearbook should offer the adviser/sponsor/coach some sort of personal reward and satisfaction. National Education Association (1980) research findings show that

> the vast majority of head sport coaches and vocal/instrumental music coaches receive extra pay for their extracurricular duties—90 and 83 percent respectively. . . . On the other hand, the vast majority of club advisors (81 percent) do not receive extra pay for their extracurricular duties. More than half of the class/grade advisors (57 percent), newspaper, yearbook, magazine advisors (56 percent), and drama/forensics/debate coaches (54 percent) receive no pay. (p. 41)

A cluster of nonteaching duties associated with teaching is implied by the school system. Individually the duties are manageable; as a cluster they consume much more time than is allowed for doing them in the school day after teaching. Some rather common nonteaching duties include

- Responding to administrative memoranda
- Completing reports or furnishing data for them
- Keeping the plan book
- Keeping student records
- Preparing and updating lesson plans
- Writing letters of recommendation
- Maintaining the instructional environment
- Promoting the program and the school

While this list is not intended to be complete, it shows the range of possible nonteaching duties and suggests how time-consuming the cluster can be.

Teacher involvement in professional and community affairs is not beyond the call of duty. It is generally encouraged and often looked upon with great favor. However, this kind of involvement usually results in a substantial investment of personal time. Professional involvement includes leadership and committee assignments in educational associations; attendance at educational conferences and conventions; making legislative contacts; writing journal articles and papers; and making speeches and presentations. Community involvement includes membership and leadership in service clubs and fraternal organizations, support of religious activities, and membership on civic committees and boards. The range of potential activity is broad and must be approached with caution. Involvement in professional or community activities can be most demanding of time to those immersed in them. The relationship to and effect on teaching must be kept in perspective at all times.

Leaves of Absence

Leaves of absence permit time away from school without threat to a position. They accommodate to such things as illness, unusual and unexpected circumstances, special professional opportunities requiring longer periods of time, maternity and child care, and study.

Letters and proposals are the common means for requesting leaves. Among other conditions, they should stipulate how the leave time is to be spent and, in the case of sabbaticals or extended leaves, the products or results that are expected. Of course, the time should be invested as stipulated. Upon the termination of the leave, it is essential that a letter or report, depending upon the length of the leave, be written and submitted to the grantor of the leave.

Descriptions of the various kinds of leaves follow. They are drawn from parts of a number of teacher agreements and contracts to illustrate the variety of purposes and the scope of time they encompass.

SICK LEAVE

Employees are commonly allowed ten sick days with pay each school year. Unused sick leave days are accumulated from year to year with no maximum limit. For teachers commencing employment after the opening of school, one sick leave day is allowed for each full month of employment. Upon retirement the teacher is commonly reimbursed at a fixed rate for the unused sick leave days accumulated during employment.

TEMPORARY LEAVES OF ABSENCE

Employees are normally entitled to temporary leaves of absence with full pay each school year. Excused absences may be requested for death in the immediate family (four days); court or military orders (unspecified time); attendance at professional meetings and conventions (four days); and personal days for business, or family illness (3 days). Unused personal days are added to the employee's accumulated sick leave. Absences for reasons that are not included in any of the preceding categories may be excused by the superintendent with loss of pay.

EXTENDED LEAVES OF ABSENCE

Leaves of absence, upon request, are often granted for such purposes as engaging in professional activities of the education association; joining the Peace Corps, Vista, or Teachers Corps; serving as an exchange teacher in a foreign country or territory of the United States; participating in a scholarship or fellowship program; serving in the military; rearing children; caring for a sick member of the immediate family; or other good cause. Federal or state appointments, political activity, and personal illness may be appropriate reasons for requesting an extended leave of absence.

MATERNITY LEAVE

The common understanding concerning maternity leaves is that they are not sick leaves and are taken without pay. They may vary in length from weeks to two years. All benefits to which the teacher was entitled at the time when the leave of absence commenced are commonly restored to her upon her return.

SABBATICAL LEAVES

A sabbatical leave is designed to help teachers improve or update themselves professionally. A sabbatical leave may be granted for purposes of advanced study, travel, or, in the case of vocational teachers, for gaining technological or industrial experience. The length of the sabbatical leave may be a half year or a full year. Time spent on sabbaticals is counted toward service increments. Teachers granted sabbaticals must generally agree to return to school for one full year after completing the leave.

Leaves of absence are bonuses of time. They are intended as grants of time to teachers to meet unusual needs and demands. Review your teaching contract for specifics. Make good use of leaves of absence; do not abuse the benefits. The abuse of leave use is not uncommon, and it is costly to school districts. Time is a valuable resource that cannot be given away by schools or accepted by teachers without some measure of accountability.

Closing Statement

Two conclusions about time, as it relates to schools and teachers, are drawn from this chapter:

1. *The teachers' school day is highly structured and rather restrictive in terms of time.* The conditions require that teachers know the duties and responsibilities of their jobs and the rules and regulations governing them if they wish to manage themselves skillfully to use their professional time well. Teachers are encouraged to search for the autonomy that remains in the organizational framework of their particular school and then take professional action to make effective use of that freedom, especially in terms of using the resource of time.
2. *The amount of time spent by teachers in school (hours per day and days per year) is less than that spent by other types of professionals in their offices.* The fact is that teachers have a generous portion of time to use outside the school day and school year. Determining how to use this time well may be perplexing, though, since, for example, the teacher's workday is longer than the school day. The teacher's workday outside of the school day may range from one to five hours. When heavy investments of time outside the school day doing schoolwork become an annoyance, the teacher should try to determine the cause of the problem. Analyze how well you are managing yourself, review your job duties and responsibilities, and examine your use of time in relation to the time usage principles and practices outlined in the remaining chapters of this book. Eliminate the annoyance by reducing the number of hours doing schoolwork outside the school day.

4
Effective Communication

> I know what I mean but I can't seem to express it. . . . It was the most, er—, well—, How shall I put this to make you see what I mean.
>
> —Harry Shaw

Unexpressed ideas are valueless. Ideas must be communicated to have worth. Words, in written and oral forms, are the principal tools for communicating. Words are symbols used to share information and to direct and control activities and processes.

The communicative process entails the sending of a message through a channel by a source to a receiver, and can be illustrated as shown in figure 4.1. The "source" is the originator of the message, which can be written, spoken, or expressed in music or another art form. The "channel" ordinarily used in teaching is verbal interaction, but the channel can also be books, films, and other instructional aids. The "receiver" is the person, class, or audience to whom the message is directed. In the classroom, the source is most often thought of as the teacher, while the receivers are thought to be the students.

FIGURE 4.1. Communicative Process

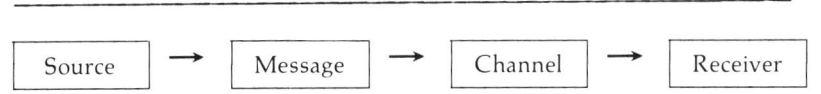

| Source | → | Message | → | Channel | → | Receiver |

Note: From American Association of Agricultural College Editors, *Communications Handbook* (Danville, Ill.: Interstate Printers and Publishers, 1976), p. 3. Reprinted by permission.

With instructional interaction, both teacher and students serve interchangeably in the two roles.

Teaching, as all good teachers know, depends exclusively on good communication to "sell" ideas and bring about change in the minds of those being taught. To communicate well requires a conscious effort by the teacher to determine what ideas he or she wishes to communicate and how they are to be presented. Frankly, much of good communication is engaging the mind in advance of opening the mouth or putting the pen to the paper. John Morgan's description of the "common denominators" of communication (figure 4.2) provides a useful review of what good communication is all about.

Poor communication often results in misunderstandings that are costly to correct in terms of time and money. The cause may be anywhere in the process and may involve any one of the four components. With that in mind, here are some potential trouble spots to look for if you wish to improve the clarity and efficiency of your teaching communications.

1. *Source.* The selection of obscure and pretentious words, Latin phrases, and technical or professional jargon is likely to create a

FIGURE 4.2. Common Denominators of Good Communication

It is more or less continuous.
It deals with both big and little matters with equal care and thoroughness.
It is concrete and specific. It shows as much as it tells.
It explains why.
It acknowledges risks and difficulties, if any, and reports steps to minimize them.
It lists benefits that could result, but lists them realistically.
It solicits questions or feedback, to help cut off the rumor mill.
It invites participation.
It avoids surprise to minimize upsetting people.
It sets standards because people want to know what's expected of them.
It contacts informal leaders.
It praises, genuinely and sincerely.
It repeats, using fresh examples, different approaches.

Note: From J.S. Morgan, "Apply Communications Wisdom," in *Communication and the Technical Professional* by Charles H. Vervalin, Editor. Copyright © 1981 by Gulf Publishing Company, Houston, Texas. All rights reserved. Used with permission.

language gap between the source and the receiver. Messages that must be decoded to be understood are risky and wasteful of time. The source would do well to anticipate the optimal level at which to communicate. Know your audience. The source can do much to minimize the problem illustrated in the trite comment, "I know that you believe you understand what you think I said, but I am not sure you realize that what you heard is not what I mean."

2. *Message.* A clear, complete, and succinct message is an objective of the source and a blessing to the receiver. Adhering to acceptable styles and formats for the various modes of communicating improves messages. There are rules for composing poetry, preparing journal articles, and writing business letters, as there are for demonstrating skills or giving persuasive speeches. Just as a recipe must be followed to make a cherry pie, so must rules be followed to prepare an exemplary message. When the policeman directs the driver of a car to "go ahead and back up," the message is succinct, but is it clear? Is it complete? The time and effort invested in the message can be expected to correlate highly with the results. Some messages pay off handsomely; others require follow-up apologies, corrections, or more information to supplement the original message. Attorneys are acutely aware of the importance of clarity and specificity in their transactions.

3. *Channel.* The more common channels for communicating in school are conversation and books. Selected television programs, addresses by distinguished speakers, guided educational tours, and modern texts and references are channels of communication with special promise of extraordinary delivery. Messages worth preparing are worth dependable and appealing means of delivery. Dated handouts, defective audiovisual equipment, and poor speakers are to be avoided.

4. *Receiver.* The communicative process is incomplete until the message is received. Readiness or openness of the receiver to the message is difficult to determine. Motivating, conditioning, and timing are techniques used to prepare the receiver to want to hear, see, or otherwise accept the message being sent. The ensuing vote, test score, or sales volume is a measure of how well the message was received. To talk if no one is listening, to write if no one is reading, or to perform if no one is watching, except for practice, is a waste of time. The communicative process requires an audience of at least one person who is ready and willing to receive the message. Mass production of the message for general consumption improves efficiency.

Gellerman (1960) suggests three basic reasons for poor internal communications:

1. A weak system for transmitting information—such as the one that moves too slowly, or which doesn't inform all people equally well, or which is so incomplete as to encourage guessing and rumor mongering.
2. Clumsy use of language—an inability to get a point across interestingly or unambiguously.
3. The tendency of people to read their own hopes and fears into things they see and hear. (pp. 236-37)

Lack of communication is also a waste of time. Waiting for an incoming class of students to settle down—without telling them to do so—is a classic example. An illustration from family life may strengthen the point. Two family members may have had expectations for each other that did not materialize because the expectations were not verbalized. Each thought the other would mail the check to pay the utility bill on time. Neither followed through. The consequences of the lack of communication were a personal trip to the utility company, an embarrassing explanation, and a penalty fee for late payment. Lack of communication can result in oversights; it can also result in duplication and waste.

Meetings

The United States is a nation of joiners. Membership organizations hold meetings because they are important to the smooth functioning of organizations. Long (1967) describes the motives for holding meetings:

They are an instrument for passing along and exchanging important information.
They may be a problem-solving device.
They give the opportunity for social contact and for the alleviation of the loneliness which most individuals feel.
They present the possibility of adding educational and cultural backgrounds, and the avowed purpose of many meetings is just that.
They may themselves accomplish or bring about the achievement of tangible ends. (p. 3)

A meeting is a gathering for a common purpose. That common purpose should be clearly delineated to the membership. Those expected to attend should receive an advance copy of the meeting program. Programs detail activities of meetings and prevent deviation, except by vote of the assembled group. The information provided by programs is useful in making the decision as to whether or not to attend the meeting (see figure 5.2).

Meetings are costly of time, and especially so when programs are without substance or are irrelevant to needs. One is justified in feeling that the time would be better spent on an activity with a higher priority. Why sit in a teachers' meeting when it offers little or nothing? What are the consequences if the required meeting is not attended or if you attend but walk out before it is adjourned? Loyalty or timidity can be costly of time and the cause of much mental anguish. The compromise is to attend or remain in the worthless teachers' meeting but use the time to do mental planning, relax, or perhaps to read.

When in charge of a meeting, start it on time, keep it on time, and end it on time. Make careful preparations. Prior to the beginning of the meeting, check the meeting room: rearrange the furniture if necessary, set up audiovisual equipment, have handouts ready, and in every way be prepared for an efficient performance. Meet and greet the guests and participants as they arrive. This practice provides the opportunity to smooth out the unwritten details of the program before the meeting is called to order.

In introducing a speaker, bear in mind that well-organized, brief introductions receive the best response from both the speaker and the audience. Presenting the highlights from a resumé is sufficient to set the stage for the speaker. Prominent speakers are usually accorded shorter introductions than are lesser known ones. Our nation's top elected leader is introduced with the straightforward statement, "Ladies and Gentlemen: the president of the United States." Lengthy introductions that draw on the insignificant can embarrass the one being introduced and often frustrate the audience. They delay the presentation and either shorten it or extend the meeting. To be appreciated when making introductions, respect brevity.

When making oral presentations, have something worthwhile to say. Next, say it so that it can be heard and understood. Deliver the message in an energetic and dynamic way. It could be what was said, how it was delivered, or both that made the presentation worthy or not worthy of the time invested. In a nutshell, these are the rules followed by speakers who value the preciousness of the other person's time.

CONDUCT OF BUSINESS MEETINGS

The final paragraph of the introduction to *Robert's Rules of Order* (1970) states:

> The application of parliamentary law is the best method yet devised to enable assemblies of any size, with due regard for every member's opinion, to arrive at the general will on a maximum number of questions of varying complexity in a minimum of time and under all kinds of internal climate ranging from total harmony to hardened or impassioned division of opinion. (p. xlii)

A set of democratic principles underlying parliamentary law includes

- Taking one item of business at a time
- The right of the minority to be heard
- Orderly discussion
- Courtesy to everyone
- Majority rule

Eighty-two motions are listed in *Robert's Rules of Order* (1970). Each motion is categorized under one of seven headings: (1) class (privileged, incidental, subsidiary), (2) if in order when another motion is on the floor, (3) whether it needs a second, (4) whether it is debatable, (5) whether it is amendable, (6) what size vote is required for adoption, and (7) whether the motion can be reconsidered. A parliamentarian is usually selected to guide the president or chairperson through the meeting. The recording secretary translates the actions of the meeting into minutes.

The following dialogue illustrates the proper procedure and language for executing a main motion in a business meeting.

CHAIR: Is there any new business?
MEMBER A *(Rises and addresses the chair)*: Mr. President.
CHAIR *(Recognizes the member by name if known)*: Mrs. Smith.
MRS. SMITH: I move that the Teachers Association present a one hundred dollar award to the class valedictorian.
MEMBER B: I second the motion.

CHAIR: It was moved and seconded that the Teachers Association present a one hundred dollar award to the class valedictorian. Is there any discussion?

MRS. SMITH (*Rises and addresses the chair*): Mr. President.

CHAIR: Mrs. Smith.

MRS. SMITH: I believe that a scholarship awards program should be started in the school. I also believe that the Teachers Association should initiate it. This is our opportunity to get it started. I strongly encourage the membership to vote for the motion.

CHAIR: Thanks, Mrs. Smith. Is there any further discussion? (*Pause*) There being no further discussion, we will vote on the motion that the Teachers Association present a one hundred dollar award to the class valedictorian. Those in favor say "aye." (*Members respond.*) Those opposed say "no." (*Members respond.*) The motion is carried. The Teachers Association will present a one hundred dollar award to the class valedictorian. (*One tap of the gavel signifies that the floor is open for the next item of business.*)

The action is recorded in the minutes as follows: "Mrs. Smith moved that the Teachers Association present a one hundred dollar award to the class valedictorian. The motion was seconded. The motion was passed (carried)."

Much of the efficiency of a meeting in which these rules are followed is credited to the exactness of the procedures, the preciseness of the language, and the focus on a single item at a time. What may seem like duplication to the novice is actually an assurance of clarity and a full airing of the motion on the floor. It is the duty of the chair to make sure that the membership is fully informed as the meeting progresses and that the meeting progresses according to the approved agenda coupled with the ongoing wishes of a majority of the membership.

Consciousness of the use of time is noticeable throughout parliamentary law. Motions to limit debate, fix time at which to adjourn, and take a recess are about use of time. To call for a division of the house, request the orders of the day, and move to reconsider a motion take additional time. They are procedures for checking on actions and progress. Their purpose is to remove doubt before proceeding. To this extent, building on a faulty foundation is averted.

Critical meetings not conducted according to parliamentary law encourage legal action. Disgruntled members may search for reasons to overturn votes, especially those relating to power structures and money matters. Business cannot be transacted without a quorum, nor is business transacted at a meeting that is not conducted according to parliamentary law likely to stand up in court. For teachers' associations and organizations with aggressive members and weighty agendas, the use of parliamentary law in meetings is a valuable safeguard. To restate the matter simply, in terms of time use: "If it is not done right, it may have to be done over."

Communicating in Class

Research findings on the subject of instructional clarity have been reported by Gephart, Strother, and Duckett (1981). They report that instructional clarity was at the top of a list of teacher behaviors that have been associated with student achievement in a significant number of research studies. Drawing upon data from three recent studies, Gephart et al. compiled a list of items that are "determiners of or related to instructional clarity." Figure 4.3 lists these items and includes a scale to measure a teacher's instructional clarity. This Instructional Clarity Checklist is a tool for improving communication between teacher and students. It may be used by the teacher as a self-evaluation instrument or may be given to students to fill out, as a means of getting instructional clarity feedback. (For student use, the information and directions would have to be written differently.) The purpose of the checklist, whether completed by the teacher or students, is to help teachers avoid vague, slipshod, and inexact instructional behavior that accounts for untold hours of wasted time in schools every year.

Reading

Teachers as a group are generally expected to be devoted readers. Teachers are counted upon to be well read and "up-to-date" about a multitude of topics and conditions. They are expected to be ready with facts and figures instantaneously.

Discounting the reasons, teachers do tend to read broadly and thoroughly. Professional reading requires much time. When reading is too costly of time, ways must be found to be a more effective and efficient reader.

The decision to read or not to read something in a report, book, or journal is yours to make. Since most of what is read is forgotten, it saves time to read only what is likely to be worth remembering. The

FIGURE 4.3. Instructional Clarity Checklist

Directions: Below are thirty-two items describing instructional behaviors that contribute to instructional clarity. To the right of these items is a scale. For each item, put a check mark at the location that best describes how often you as a teacher perform the instructional behaviors. The scale is as follows:

4 All of the time   1 Never
3 Most of the time   0 Does not apply
2 Some of the time

	4	3	2	1	0
1. Explains the work to be done and how to do it	( )	( )	( )	( )	( )
2. Asks students before they start work if they know what to do and how to do it.	( )	( )	( )	( )	( )
3. Explains something, then stops so student can think about it	( )	( )	( )	( )	( )
4. Takes time when explaining	( )	( )	( )	( )	( )
5. Orients and prepares students for what is to follow	( )	( )	( )	( )	( )
6. Provides students with standards and rules for satisfactory performance	( )	( )	( )	( )	( )
7. Specifies content and shares overall structure for the lectures with students	( )	( )	( )	( )	( )
8. Helps students to organize materials in a meaningful way	( )	( )	( )	( )	( )
9. Repeats questions and explanations if students don't understand	( )	( )	( )	( )	( )
10. Repeats and stresses directions and difficult points	( )	( )	( )	( )	( )
11. Encourages and lets students ask questions	( )	( )	( )	( )	( )
12. Answers students' questions	( )	( )	( )	( )	( )
13. Provides practice time	( )	( )	( )	( )	( )
14. Synthesizes ideas and demonstrates real-world relevancy	( )	( )	( )	( )	( )
15. Adjusts teaching to the learner and the topic	( )	( )	( )	( )	( )
16. Teaches at a pace appropriate to the topic and students	( )	( )	( )	( )	( )
17. Personalizes instruction by using many teaching strategies	( )	( )	( )	( )	( )
18. Continuously monitors student learning and adjusts instructional strategy to the needs of the learner	( )	( )	( )	( )	( )

FIGURE 4.3 (continued)

		4	3	2	1	0
19.	Teaches in a related, step-by-step manner	( )	( )	( )	( )	( )
20.	Uses demonstrations	( )	( )	( )	( )	( )
21.	Uses a variety of teaching materials	( )	( )	( )	( )	( )
22.	Provides illustrations and examples	( )	( )	( )	( )	( )
23.	Emphasizes the key terms/ideas to be learned	( )	( )	( )	( )	( )
24.	Consistently reviews work as it is completed and provides students with feedback or knowledge of results	( )	( )	( )	( )	( )
25.	Insures that students have an environment in which they are encouraged to process what they are learning	( )	( )	( )	( )	( )
26.	Makes clear transitions	( )	( )	( )	( )	( )
27.	Reduces mazes	( )	( )	( )	( )	( )
28.	Avoids vague terms	( )	( )	( )	( )	( )
29.	Avoids fillers (uh, ah, um)	( )	( )	( )	( )	( )
30.	Reduces nonessential content	( )	( )	( )	( )	( )
31.	Communicates so that all students can understand	( )	( )	( )	( )	( )
32.	Demonstrates a high degree of verbal fluency	( )	( )	( )	( )	( )

Note: From William Gephart, Deborah B. Strother, and Williard R. Duckett, eds., Practical Applications of Research, newsletter of Phi Delta Kappa's Center on Evaluation, Development, and Research, Bloomington, Ill., 3 (March 1981), 3. The scale was added to the Center's list. Adapted with permission.

insignificance or irrelevance of some things makes them worthless as reading materials.

Most agree that reading junk mail is a waste of time. There are those who throw it in the trash can without taking the time to open it. Opening it takes time, too.

A newspaper read from front to back is another waste of time. It is a good idea to limit the amount of time you wish to spend reading the newspaper and stick by the decision. Is there a reason to read the obituaries or classified ads daily, or has the practice become a time-consuming habit?

Be selective of the articles read in technical and professional journals. First, read those articles with immediate payoff. If the journal is written around a theme of little interest to you, disregard it completely.

Lengthy books and research reports do not always have to be read word for word, from beginning to end, to meet a need. To do so can be wasteful of time. Your approach to skimming such materials will depend upon the purpose of the reading.

Glance through the materials to get an overview. In a book, the table of contents and introduction provide clues to structure and essence. Meaningful, as opposed to catchy, headings and subheadings are useful to the skimmer. Topic sentences contain the heart of each paragraph and, when well written, accommodate skimming.

Make a wide, sweeping search to locate the specific information you are after in the material you are reading. Turn to the index of a book or abstract of a piece of research to determine if further explorations might be profitable. The next step is to pick and choose more specific pieces of information, or quotations, that support the major theoretical points and add to the clarity and completeness of your understanding.

One could read twenty-four hours a day for a lifetime and still read only a fraction of what has been printed. It is speculated that the proliferation of the printed word is such that it requires a disciplined reader to keep up in any area of specialization. One recourse is to disregard some materials immediately and choose from among the remainder according to your needs.

Vary reading speed with the kind of materials being read and the purpose of reading them. Savor a novel, ponder a problem, and study a lesson; assimilate directions, comprehend a report, evaluate a test, review a book, check an order, and scrutinize research. Each suggests a style of reading. Pausing and rereading are necessary at times. When reading relates to safety, finances, and legal matters, full understanding is given precedence over reading speed. Fast reading is a time-saver at times. When it is likely to result in accidents, poor decisions, and injustices, it may well be a time-waster and cannot be condoned.

Writing

According to Shaw,

> Reading and writing are two aspects of the same process—the communication of thoughts, moods and emotions. When you write effectively you convey your ideas and feelings to others; when you

read well you receive from others their ideas and feelings. Since reading and writing are inseparably linked, it is important that in trying to learn to write well you learn to read well. (Shaw, 1945, bk. 3, p. 3)

RULES AND REFERENCE RESOURCES

Before writing, know the guides and rules that dictate reasonable acceptance of the written product. Elements of style and discipline differ among the various kinds of written materials. It is often a matter of either meeting the established criteria or having the product doomed to failure, which is not gratifying personally, nor is it the best use of time.

Also prior to writing, surround yourself with the appropriate reference sources. A dictionary, thesaurus, and a grammar handbook are minimum resources. Style manuals and the publisher's or grantor's individualized guidelines are necessary too. Having the right technical aids at hand is a kind of reinforcement. It somehow makes the task easier to accomplish and tends to improve the end product.

Finally, think before you write. Errors of thought are reflected in errors of writing. Clear and well-defined thoughts result in clear and crisp writing. Write what you care and know about. Knowing and caring result in more dynamic articles, reports, memos, or anything else that is written.

Write simply. Select the important, reject the unimportant, and arrange logically that which remains. Make a point, support it if necessary, and go on to the next point. Cover the subject, but in doing so, keep the message short. Brevity is appreciated.

TRIM TIME-WASTERS

The ways to reduce writing time are generally known—but not widely practiced—by teachers. When the practice takes preparatory time or a system to make it operable, it is unlikely to be used, even though it promises to be a long-term time-saver.

Business correspondence is a likely first place to trim. For example, do not thank someone for a "thank you" letter. It is not necessary. When letters are required, consider individualized form letters or letters constructed from a pool of modular statements. The standardized form letter can be used again and again with two or three individualized insertions, which are easy to do with modern word processing equipment. The form letter is ideal for renting films and ordering instructional materials. A variation of the standard form letter is to store a number of carefully prepared paragraphs in a memory device of a typewriter for future letter writing. Writing time is reduced by drawing on the stored paragraphs.

Make liberal use of carbon copies or photocopies to keep peripheral people informed. One well-drafted letter, with three copies, can serve four people better than four individualized letters. Secondly, it is a commonly accepted practice to answer a letter by penning a legible note on the bottom of the page, having the letter photocopied, and returning it in that form. The penned note is personal, and it is fast. It is fast because all that remains to be done is to address an envelope and mail the letter. If the style appears objectionable, the swift turnaround time more than compensates for it.

Writing an examination can take too generous a chunk of time right when one seems to need it most. One way of getting around this major expenditure of time is not to write an examination. Instead, write test items or questions. A test item can be written during spare minutes and another when more minutes are available, and so on. At examination time it is most likely that you will have accumulated a pool of test items of sufficient size for three or four examinations. Now that the items are written, categorize them and randomly select the desired number from each category. Sequence the test items and have a teacher's aide or secretary type them into an examination format. When the examination is typed, return the test items to the original pool. Each year add new items to the pool as the supply for new examinations, with little effort and little writing.

Cut writing time by using quantities of brochures, handouts, diagrams, and maps to provide information, answer requests, and give directions or instructions. Messages that are used frequently and in large numbers should be well written and appropriately packaged to supplement and, in many cases, prevent the necessity for additional writing. Readily available supplies of a variety of information pieces pare writing time dramatically. For instance, a brochure and a form letter can answer a first request about an academic program; a map and an agenda can pinpoint location and specify time of a meeting; a handout can explain a complicated or detailed process or procedure. Make generous use of your professional business cards by attaching them to materials, with or without a short personal note.

There are a number of other ways of cutting the writing time for teaching activities. For example, when preparing annual reports, refer to previous reports for general and historical information or format. Consider purchasing a major portion of your teaching aids rather than preparing them. In lieu of writing a newspaper article about a school activity, invite a reporter and photographer to cover the event.

Shorten a proposed journal article or professional paper by 25 to 50 percent. Not only will writing time be pared; the tasks are likely to be completed earlier and be of better quality.

Listening

The world of today is a listening world. While reading and writing are emphasized in the school curriculum, it is listening and speaking that are used most often by the average person. Of the four language arts, listening is the most frequently used communication skill.

Listening involves hearing, but it is more than that. Petrie (1966) used the term to mean "the composite process by which oral language communicated by some source is received, critically and purposefully attended to, recognized, and interpreted (or comprehended) in terms of past experiences and future expectancies" (p. 329). Listening demands sustained attention. The spoken message usually passes by only once, unless it is recorded; repeat messages are uncommon.

PITFALLS OF LISTENING COMPREHENSION

Dover (1966, p. 369) observes that "deficiencies in listening skill carry with them an extremely high and needless price tag in both time and dollars." He lists seven pitfalls to listening comprehension:

1. Don't let the details of what you hear obscure the speaker's central theme.
2. Don't let your mind wander to other matters while listening to someone talk.
3. Don't let your built-in emotional filter distort the listening process.
4. Don't let the listening environment interfere with listening efficiency.
5. Don't let excessive note taking diminish your listening effectiveness.
6. Don't overlook opportunities to improve your listening through practice.
7. Don't reject what you hear because it appears to be trivial, completely familiar, or completely unfamiliar. (pp. 377-81)

GOOD LISTENING HABITS

Constructive and purposeful listening is learned. Learn to turn pitfalls into productive listening habits. To comprehend oral presentations more fully,

1. *Focus attention on the central theme.* If nothing else, remember the theme. It was the issue, the concern that was all-important in the message delivered. Themes are usually developed in terms of from three to five subordinate points, which in turn are supported with specific details. Depending on the type of presentation—sermon, lecture, commencement address—many will have forgotten the supporting details in a few hours, the main points concerning the theme in a few days, and the theme itself in a few weeks. Unless the message made a lasting impression or served an immediately useful purpose, it is difficult to justify the time invested in listening.
2. *Keep up with the message as it is presented.* The technique is mind control. It is easy to muse over the speaker's language, grammar, or delivery at the expense of listening. It is easy to think about matters at school or home rather than listening to the speaker. Why be physically present and mentally absent? If the intent was to hear the message, then listen intently. Using part of the time to listen to the message and part of the time to think about other things is not good use of time for either purpose. It is difficult, if not impossible, to serve two masters well.
3. *Be aware that personal bias or deep-seated opinion can interfere with listening.* Preconceptions about the topic or presenter can block or abet listening. Just the realization of differences between "thee and me" can reduce the influence of emotion on the message. Building a case against or in support of the message during the presentation is not listening. Whatever it is, it hinders listening. A good listening habit is to be open and receptive to the message. Assimilate it as it is presented; assess it upon its completion.
4. *Tune out or minimize environmental distractions.* Loud music from next door, an uncomfortably warm room, a ringing telephone on the wall, the overhead noise of a passing plane, and a host of other conditions can disrupt even an attentive listener. Every conceivable environmental distraction possible should be considered and anticipated prior to an oral presentation. As a listener, you have options. Move away from heat or draft if uncomfortable. Stay clear of a busy exit or entrance. Request the noisy person next to you to be quiet so you can hear. Best of all, keep the distance between the speaker and yourself, the listener, at a minimum to solve most of the environmental problems. Physical closeness crowds out environmental distractions. It seems to motivate the listener to be more attentive as well.
5. *Limit note taking.* If it is done for purposes of recall, it substitutes hearing for listening. Note taking emphasizes details at the ex-

pense of the theme. Attempting to listen and write simultaneously results in gaps in listening and occasionally in inaccurate notes. Depend on the original document for the recipe being read, the poem being recited, or the steps in the process being enumerated. Take notes sparingly; excessive note taking diminishes listening effectiveness.

6. *Improve listening skill.* Practice the art with the help of a friend who is also interested in improving his or her listening skill. Try using a role reversal technique. The procedure is as follows: (1) listen to the other person speak; (2) repeat the directions, argument, or story; (3) continue until the other person is satisfied that you have an understanding of the message; (4) reverse roles and repeat the technique using a new topic. This technique is without threat. It provides immediate feedback, and it also indirectly reflects the clarity with which the person who is speaking presents the message.

7. *Be receptive to the simple and the complex, the new and the old.* Understanding can come from many levels and perspectives. The complex, when understood, is simple; the old, when updated, takes on newness. To illustrate, an agriculture teacher used one meeting each winter, for three years, to explain to young farmers the procedures and practices necessary to produce quality eggs. When the young farmers questioned the repetition of old information and simple practices at the fourth winter meeting, they were quickly informed that either they had not been listening to the previous presentations or they were not following through—for they were not producing quality eggs in accordance with established standards. Receptivity can be, and generally is, evaluated by the teacher. Receptivity values the message associated with the talking/listening process.

Talking

According to William A. Ward, "The mediocre teacher tells. The good teacher explains. The superior teacher demonstrates. The great teacher inspires."

Most teachers depend heavily on talking to fulfill their professional role. Teacher talk is costly of time in the classroom. More important, it is what teachers say and how they say it that makes the difference between a mediocre and a great teacher. Talking time is not used well when teachers

- Impart inaccurate and outdated information
- Ramble without lesson plans or benefit of notes
- Lecture at the expense of the more productive methods of instruction
- Stretch lessons with filler materials such as irrelevant stories or jokes and insignificant details

These abuses of time have no place in the classroom. The cure for the first three is preclass planning. A remedy for the latter is to terminate unproductive talk by making a meaningful assignment and supervising student study. Most teachers recognize when talking is futile; the master teacher does something about it.

To lecture is to talk. The lecture, in itself, is not generally the best use of teaching time, simply because most students tire of it shortly after it begins. Use it sparingly to introduce or summarize a topic or describe an experience. Use it primarily to support other methods of instruction. Talk supported with concrete experiences is more productive of learning than is talk alone. Limit the time used to lecture.

One technique used to study a chain of classroom events involving verbal communications is *interaction analysis*. Flanders (1970) describes interaction analysis as "a label that refers to any technique for studying the chain of classroom events in such a fashion that each event is taken into consideration" (p. 5). After many years of research in interaction analysis, he reached the following conclusions about teacher talk:

> By way of summarizing the current state of affairs in our classrooms, it does not seem very far out of line to suggest that teachers usually tell pupils what to do, how to do it, when to start, when to stop, and how well they did whatever they did. (p. 14)
>
> While it is true that teachers talk more than all pupils combined, from kindergarten to graduate school, the major problem appears not to lie in the quantity, but in the quality. . . . Very little teacher talk is devoted to a consideration of ideas or opinions expressed by the pupils; their ideas are not dealt with adequately. (p. 13)
>
> By judiciously adapting teacher behavior to the various teaching situations, a small increase in the proportion of time devoted to responding to pupil ideas seems to be associated with an increased pupil growth in both subject matter and positive attitude. (p. 424)

Closing Statement

Teaching is largely talking, reading, writing, and listening. Since a preponderance of the teacher's time is spent in these activities, it is reasonable to assume that it is here that great savings can be made. Improving your use of time when applying communications skills in the teaching process not only benefits your teaching but also improves your ability to practice these skills. Excellence in teaching is heavily dependent upon success in communication.

Instructional clarity is a powerful force when dealing with students in the classroom. It infers the use of lesson plans, the selection of teaching strategies that personalize the message, encouragement of student participation, and the skillful creation of tests to aid students to perform well. Teaching that results in little or no learning is a waste of both teachers' and students' time. Adopting and practicing teacher behaviors that contribute to instructional clarity is an important way of improving your use of teacher time in the classroom.

Meetings, occasions arranged for passing along or exchanging information, engaging in problem-solving activity, and for similar kinds of interaction, are intended to promote communication but do not always achieve this goal. Teachers spend much precious time in many prolonged meetings that are of questionable value to them. Some meetings are unnecessary. Many of the essential ones are poorly planned or are not conducted with dispatch. Written agendas, prepared speakers, and parliamentary procedures improve the quality and shorten the time of business meetings. Excessive, irrelevant, and drawn-out meetings are an infringement on teachers' time. Resist them.

5
Programming Activity

> To everything there is a season, and a time to every purpose under heaven.
> —Ecclesiastes

Programming is regarded in this chapter as a "what" and "when" regimen. It is the mental exercise of determining the activities and events that are to be done and then scheduling them for attainment or achievement. The "what" precedes the "when." Planning the kinds of activities and events is of primary concern; scheduling them is secondary. Projecting into the future by planning and scheduling is the initial step in making commitments.

Programming is not crucial to those who have given little thought to time as a precious resource. Educators, unlike business persons and industrialists, do not stress the criticality of time in their work. Arlin (1979), an educational psychologist, studied teachers' perception of time and concluded that "the economic notion of time as a scarce resource to be allocated with care seemed foreign to most teachers. Many seemed to view time as something to be used up or even 'to kill' rather than to 'spend wisely'" (p. 53).

In considering the question "What margin for instructional change exists in the high school?" Cuban (1982) pointed out how difficult it is for teachers to look beyond the events of the busy teaching day in order to program activities for the future:

> With the current school day sliced into periods of less than an hour, with teachers facing between 125 and 170 students a day in batches of 25 to 35, with a teaching load of five classes and two or more different lesson preparations, with a dozen other external require-

ments of grading, credits, and exams—with all of these structural givens, the margin for change is terribly slim. The organizational load and the structure within which teachers work—when wedded to their isolation from peers and sporadic supervision—mean that far too many teachers complete a school day without once reflecting with colleagues on what pedagogy was used in classes, what mistakes and successes occurred, or a dozen other professional issues that arise and disappear in the complicated discourse and action that unfold in a 50-minute period. Widening the margin for change would mean modifying teachers' class loads, their amount of contact time with students, or any of a vast number of other structural variables. (p. 117)

If programming is not vital to the teacher in teaching, it is not likely to be vital to the teacher in nonteaching roles. Given this condition, attention to programming must be directed to the whole being and with undaunted vigor. A respect for time as a resource usually grows out of positive experiences in planning and scheduling. Written lists are, in a sense, commitments to follow through on each item. Programming gives positive direction to one's life. But it does more than that. It sparks action that yields results in return simply for living one's life. Accomplishments attest to the value of programming and reinforce the practice. The cycle has a way of energizing itself.

Planning

Planning is envisioning a way of doing something or achieving an end. It always implies mental formulation. Good planning begins with objectives and goals; it culminates in a written list, inventory, or blueprint intended to chart direction and initiate activity.

Planning is to time as budgeting is to money. Unlike money, a full share of time is due you, and no more. The certain but inelastic supply of time must be sufficient to permit you to do the things you want to do. The amount of time is fixed; how it is used becomes the variable. Planning, motivated by enlightened self-interest, is a means of generating personalized agendas loaded with high-priority activities and events. Planning helps one get at the important things.

The reward underlying planning is the high returns in achievement, realization, and productivity. Well-conceived plans advance you toward goals in life. They inspire you to do the important things, bring about positive change, and make an impressive impact at school, in the community, and at home. Indirectly, planning and plans make life exciting and living a challenge.

Teachers without plans are like builders without blueprints. Both are uncertain about what it is they are to be doing. Both are likely to hesitate at first and then begin to deal with insignificant bits and pieces of the job. Anything more would be overwhelming. While plans may not be regarded by many as necessary, they do have a way of putting the planner in control. Plans accentuate the vital and touch on the innovative things to do. At the same time, they minimize the trivial and the routine. Simply put, that is what planning, as it relates to living and teaching, is all about.

TAKE TIME TO PLAN

Planning takes time, but it also saves time. Management specialists say that time spent in planning is more than compensated for in efficiency of actual execution. Mackenzie and Lekan (1977) report that taking a "quiet hour" to think and plan can "save you up to two hours each day" (p. 10). Dillon (1983) summed up his point of view by stating that "just ten minutes of planning daily can save you ten percent of your total daily work time" (p. 4).

Time for planning must be scheduled if planning is to happen. Make appointments with yourself to plan. Do it on a regular basis and as often as necessary. Some plan for each day at the beginning of the day; others use the end of the workday to plan for the next day. Fifteen minutes and longer periods of time are set aside for thinking and listing tasks and proposed activities that will require a chunk of time. Planning is most productive when done in a quiet, comfortable setting without any interruptions. Daily plans often take the form of a "things to do" checklist. Planning research proposals, meeting agendas, and lesson plans are common duties of teachers. Guides for planning research proposals, meeting agendas, and lesson plans are outlined in figures 5.1, 5.2, and 5.3.

THE DAILY PLAN

A daily plan is a listing of things you must, should, and could do during the day, along with an estimate of the amount of time needed to do each thing and the appointed time to begin it. First, list the activities and events (other than classes that are already scheduled) on a piece of ruled tablet paper or a form prepared for the purpose.

(continued on page 70)

FIGURE 5.1. Guide for Planning Research Proposals

Know and follow funding guidelines
Introduce research problem
Provide needs statement
Define significant or technical terms
List objectives of study
Establish theoretical framework through literature
   search
Formulate questions to be answered or hypotheses to be
   tested
Define sample
Prepare or select measures for gathering data
Defend validity and reliability of data-gathering
   instruments
Set forth procedures for collecting data
Describe proposed data analysis procedures
List references used for literature search
Describe institutional resources available to researcher
Propose names of research team and provide resumés
Estimate time needed to complete project
Suggest procedures for disseminating findings
Prepare estimated budget
Append letters of endorsement

FIGURE 5.2. Guide for Planning a Meeting Agenda

---

1. Meeting called to order: may or may not include
   opening ceremony
2. Reading and approval of minutes of previous meeting
3. Treasurer's report and reports of other officers,
   as appropriate
4. Reading of communications
5. Committee reports--executive, standing, special
   committee reports, in that order
6. Unfinished business
   a.
   b.
7. New business
   a.
   b.
   c.
   d.
8. Announcements
9. Program
10. Adjournment: may or may not include closing cere-
    mony

FIGURE 5.3. Guide for Creating a Lesson Plan

Step	Specific Plan	Purpose
I. Unit:	Economics	
II. Problem:	Marketing products	
III. Situation:	The economic condition of the producer is influenced by the market. Marketing is a meeting of the minds by the producer and consumer on the true value of the product.	Creating specific situations puts the teacher in control.
IV. Objectives:	1. To know about the many methods of marketing products. 2. To be familiar with markets in the local area. 3. To understand the major factors that regulate market prices.	Unit should begin with objectives to provide concrete direction from the start.
V. Learning activities	1. Trace a product from the time it leaves the producer until it is purchased by the consumer. 2. List the kinds of markets in the local region. 3. Visit wholesale markets, and observe how they operate. 4. Listen to guest speakers discuss the role of cooperatives in marketing products.	Specifying important learning activities keeps unit on track.
VI. Assignments:	Have the students describe the services performed by each of the kinds of markets discussed.	
VII. Follow-up:	Keep a daily log of market prices for a product for one season. Give reasons for fluctuations in price or unusual prices.	Well-planned follow-ups yield high returns in student achievement and, therefore, in teacher productivity.

69

Your list might look like this:

- Meet with the principal
- Pick up groceries
- Order instructional film
- Mimeograph handouts/answer mail
- Call automobile mechanic
- Prepare weekly lesson schedule
- Attend school basketball game

After a list is created, rank the priority of each activity as something you *must* do, *should* do, or *could* do. Keep your written goals and objectives before you when prioritizing activities. Next, estimate the amount of time each activity is expected to require and mark it down. Finally, record the time of day when each activity or event is to be started. A useful format for such a Daily Planning Guide is shown in figure 5.4.

The Daily Planning Guide is revealing. It brings to light the variety and complexity of activities and events, work load, possible scheduling conflicts, and the extent of movement toward realization of goals. It provides the information required to schedule the day.

Scheduling

Scheduling follows closely upon and often actually overlaps with planning. When or where one function ends and the other begins is indistinguishable, but these two programming functions have been treated separately here for the sake of clarity. While planning is the envisioning of activities with an expectation of achieving them, scheduling is the assigning of fixed future dates and times to the envisioned activities for the purpose of initiating, implementing, and completing them. Simply stated, scheduling helps you get through the day, week, and year in a structured and an orderly fashion. It facilitates getting a quota of things done and on time.

A Daily Schedule is made up of selected activities and events from the Daily Planning Guide. It is likely that some planned activities cannot be scheduled, either because the plan was too ambitious or activities are in competition for the same time slots on the schedule. The selected activities are arranged in chronological order in accordance with the fixed appointment times.

FIGURE 5.4. Daily Planning Guide

Name		Day and Date	
Activities and Events	Importance	Time Demand	Appointment Time
Meet with principal	Must do	30 min.	8:00 a.m.
Pick up groceries	Must do	30 min.	4:00 p.m.
Order instructional film	Should do	15 min.	8:30 a.m.
Mimeograph handouts/ answer mail	Should do	15 min.	8:45 a.m.
Call automobile mechanic	Should do	10 min.	7:00 a.m.
Prepare weekly lesson schedule	Must do	45 min.	2:30 p.m.
Attend school basketball game	Could do	120 min.	7:30 p.m.

Note: At this point items are listed in the same order they were thought of, not by priority or chronologically.

It is recommended that the schedule be written on a four-by-six-inch index card, with mimeographed time designations on the left and spaces for activities and events on the right. The index cards are handy to carry in pocket or purse and are readily available. They inform you at a glance about where you should be and what you should be doing. An example of a Daily Schedule for the morning is shown in figure 5.5.

Depending upon such personal characteristics as your inclination to attend to details and to orient yourself toward either carrying out activities or following a time schedule, you may use the Daily Planning Guide, Daily Schedule, or both to help you through the day in an organized way. On either instrument, strike each item from the list as soon as it has been accomplished. Striking the item is both an immediate reward and a stimulus to complete the remainder of the tasks outlined. Seeing the plan or schedule being diminished with checked-off completions is the means for assessing how well the day is being used. Good days don't just happen; they are planned, and the plans are executed. In the words of Stellar (1973), "Success in education is almost never the result of sheer luck. It is, instead, the outcome of careful planning" (p. 12).

Some tips for preparing schedules follow.

FIGURE 5.5. Daily Schedule: Morning

Name	Day and Date
6:00 a.m.	Have breakfast/listen to news
6:30	Plan for day/clean typewriter
7:00	Call automobile mechanic/have car inspected
7:30	Commute to school
8:00	Meet with principal
8:30	Order film/mimeograph handouts/answer mail
9:00	Teach class
9:30	Teach class
10:00	Teach class
10:30	Teach class
11:00	Teach class
11:30	Teach class
12:00	Have lunch with guidance counselor

1. *Build flexibility into schedules.* Allow time for fun, pleasure, rest, exercise, and professional improvement, as well as for teaching. If you happen to be a perfectionist, allow time for perfection. And always allow time for the unexpected. A portion of your time will be consumed by such things as emergencies, interruptions, and other unanticipated circumstances. It usually takes longer than scheduled to complete the report, write the article, answer the questionnaire, and grade the papers.

   Avoid tension by allowing enough time to get the job done, to be on time, and to have breaks between appointments. If the schedule is too tight as prepared, drop a low-priority item or two to reduce the pressure.

2. *Match tasks to your energy cycle and level.* Maximize your "prime time." If you do your best teaching in the morning hours, have your preparation period and study hall scheduled for the afternoon, when possible. Tackle the difficult tasks when you are at your very best. To some it is during early morning; to some it is late in the evening, while others peak in the middle of the day.

   Mix pleasant activities with the unpleasant, easy tasks with difficult ones, and routine chores with new and innovative jobs. Variety is said to be the spice of life. It takes monotony out of the schedule.

   Schedule no more than a reasonable day's activity for the day. Overloads discourage even the most motivated of individuals. Overloads that occur day after day with no sign of relenting can cause illness.

3. *Bunch activities that can be done as a unit.* Make the trip pay. For example, go to lunch, pick up the mail, do the copying, and discuss an expected phone call with the secretary in the central office before returning to the classroom at the other end of the building. Bunching the activities is more efficient use of time than making three individual trips and an interoffice call to accomplish the same tasks.

   Grouping a number of appointments during a period of the day in the same geographical location of town saves travel time. Errands tend to cluster and can be handled as a unit in a scheduled block of time.

   Combine an education conference in a distant city with a weekend vacation. Gaining both professional enrichment and a reprieve from daily routine is making the most of a situation with a minimal additional investment.

4. *Favor high-payoff, high-priority activities.* Henry David Thoreau wrote, "It is not enough to be busy, so are ants. The question is: What are we busy about?" To move from theory to practice, why spend time making Thanksgiving holiday decorations for the classroom when the students enjoy the activity and learn by doing it?

   We all have a tendency to clean up piddling little tasks before tackling a major assignment. People are also inclined to do things they do well at the expense of other activities. The quesion of how much the activity chosen will contribute to a valued goal seems to be secondary. These tendencies are unconscious inducements to stray from what is best to what is satisfying.

   Finally, as mentioned earlier, schedule time each day to plan. Planning is among the highest of the high-payoff, high-priority activities.

5. *Use memory joggers.* It is not unusual to learn about activities and events that have been planned and scheduled by organizations months into the future. Personal scheduling must take into consideration advanced scheduling of such activities.

   Activities planned ahead for the current year can be logged into the annual appointment calendar. Those events projected further into the future can be recalled through tickler or action files. For short-term reminders, three-by-five-inch index cards are excellent for note taking. They supplement a daily "to do" list and are useful in recalling events for future scheduling.

   Without memory joggers, activities and events can easily be overlooked. An oversight cannot be rectified, since time cannot be turned back. Opportunities that elude the schedule are lost.

Closing Statement

Programming is planning and scheduling activities around the resource of time. While in theory, planning precedes scheduling, in practice the two functions are often done in concert. Those who view time as the precious resource it is are likely to plan and schedule. Programming has much to offer the teacher as a professional and as a person. The process gives direction, incites action, and pays off generously in accomplishments and satisfaction.

Planning is a mental exercise that helps one get to the important things in life. It is a means of generating personalized agendas with goal-oriented activities. Plans put you more in control of your life.

Scheduling time infers explicit activity at an appointed time and place. *Sometime* and *anytime* are terms that are vague and useless to planners. Opportunities shrouded in vague terminology are likely to be bungled. Ambiguous and nebulous scheduling can be as bad and actually worse than no scheduling at all.

6
Delegation

> No-nonsense delegation is delegation *by* objectives and *for* results.
> —Dale D. McConkey

The Concept

What is delegation? It is getting things done through others or turning things over to others who have been trained to handle them. In essence, it is the act of entrusting one's authority to another. Rutherford (1978) defines delegation as "assigning job duties to another without giving up responsibility for them" (p. 109). Definitions alone, however, do not articulate the concept fully.

Mackenzie (1972) explains delegation as a vital tool of the effective manager. He writes:

> Managing is generally defined as getting things done through people. Delegation essentially is giving people things to do. Thus by definition the two are inextricably interwoven. We must conclude that a manager who does not delegate is not managing. Of course, since there are degrees of effectiveness, a more precise statement would be that one who cannot delegate effectively cannot manage effectively. (p. 122)[1]

---

[1]Reprinted, by permission of the publisher, from THE TIME TRAP by R. Alec MacKenzie, p. 122. © 1972 by AMACOM, a division of American Management Associations, New York. All rights reserved.

Teachers are managers of instruction at school, managers of family affairs at home, and managers of organizations when in leadership positions. As such they are expected to share a part of their managerial duties with others. Delegation is a management skill; it can be beneficial to both the delegator and the delegatee.

Why Delegate?

There are a number of reasons why teachers, as managers of instruction, should delegate. Judicious delegation

- Frees the teacher to do work that cannot be delegated
- Increases the teacher's productivity
- Stresses controlling functions and deemphasizes doing them
- Provides opportunities for others to develop new skills and initiative

Why Teachers Fail to Delegate

While it is recognized that good delegation is advantageous to all involved in the process, many teachers fail to delegate except in limited ways. Among the reasons why teachers do not delegate are that they

- Believe they can do the job faster than others and are unwilling to wait for uncertain results
- Lack confidence in others' work and cannot tolerate less than high-quality results
- Fear being disliked, losing control of the position, or that delegation is not the right thing to do
- Think it is easier to do something oneself than to tell others to do it and are convinced that delegating burdens more than it benefits
- Lack the training necessary to delegate well and do not realize they can delegate to all kinds and levels of people in and out of the school
- Feel delegation reveals a level of incompetence and feel insecure when dependent upon others
- Want to account for only themselves and do not want to be indebted to others

- Believe "teaching is for teachers," are willing to accept the work load, and are unwilling to give up the necessary authority

How to Delegate

To delineate the full import of delegation, one management expert (McConkey, 1974) has compared it to a legal contract: "Just as in a legal contract, the parties (the superior and the subordinate in this instance) to the delegation (the contract) must reach a meeting of the minds as to the content and meaning of the contract's provisions." The provisions include

1. Agreement on the scope of the job (responsibility)
2. Agreement on specific results the subordinate is to achieve (accountability)
3. Agreement on the time schedule
4. Agreement on the authority needed to carry out the delegation
5. Agreement on means used to measure performance (control and feedback)
6. Agreement that the superior and subordinate each accepts his [or her] part of the contract and will live up to it. (p. 47)

In deciding which activities to delegate, the time-conscious teacher divides in-school work into several categories:

- Low-priority items that can be consigned to a shelf, drawer, or waste can
- Teaching that can be done through automated devices such as projectors, television sets, or computers
- Assignments that can be performed by students, assistants, and volunteer workers
- Projects and activities that the teacher must do

In essence, the teacher culls items with low payoffs, allocates some teaching to mechanical servants, and delegates some activities to others on the team. Finally, the professional does those things that others cannot do. Delegating, done deliberately, improves teaching and learning and therefore strengthens the position of the teacher. Entrusting rewarding assignments to others can be done without losing control of the professional position.

The assignments that others are given may be simple tasks, or they may be complex and complicated projects. The instructions accompanying assignments at the several levels of difficulty should vary accordingly. Sullivan (1980) lists four steps in the process of effective delegation;

1. Give a clear description of the task and its components.
2. Check to see that your instructions are understood; ask the other person to repeat your request.
3. Set a deadline for completion, but be sure to establish interim checkpoints as a guard against last-minute disaster.
4. Focus on results, not the methods, and allow for mistakes. (p. 6)

TIPS ON DELEGATING

Now that we have examined the steps involved in delegating, let's refine the procedure by considering some of the specific "do's and don'ts" of delegating.

When delegating, *do*

- Provide the necessary resources (along with the assignment) to get the job done
- Describe the product or results anticipated at the time when the task is delegated
- Reward those who perform well

When delegating, *do not*

- Pile assignment on top of assignment (Avoid overdelegation.)
- Delegate with strings attached (Give the authority necessary to do the job.)
- Meddle after the assignment is made (Meddling stifles initiative; it makes people nervous.)
- Delegate if it appears you may lose control
- Delegate tasks that require the element of secrecy
- Delegate to shun responsibility (The delegator is still responsible for the results of tasks assigned to others.)

GUIDELINES FOR BETTER DELEGATION

Useful guidelines for better delegation, presented by Douglass (1979, p. 60) are shown in figure 6.1. Each of the six basic guidelines

FIGURE 6.1. Guidelines for Better Delegation

1. Analyze Your Job
  a. What are your objectives?
  b. What results are expected of you?
  c. What do you do?
  d. Can anyone else do it for you?
  e. Can anyone be trained to do it?
  f. Discuss job analysis with your superiors to obtain agreement or working consensus.

2. Decide What To Delegate
  a. Decisions you make most often.
  b. Functions that make you "over-specialized."
  c. Areas in which your staff are better qualified.
  d. Areas you dislike — but remember to delegate both the good and the bad.
  e. Areas in which subordinates need development.
  f. Things that will add variety to subordinate's job.

3. Plan the Delegation
  a. Strive for "whole job" unity.
  b. Review all essential details and decisions.
  c. Clarify appropriate limits of authority.
  d. Establish performance standards.
  e. Determine appropriate feedback controls, including what information is needed, how often, and in what form.
  f. Provide for training, coaching, or back-up people.
  g. If you can't control it, don't delegate it.

4. Select the Right Person
  a. Consider interests and abilities.
  b. What degree of challenge?
  c. Who needs it most?
  d. Try to balance and rotate teams.

5. Make the Delegation
  a. Clarify the results intended and the priorities involved.
  b. Clarify degree of authority and other operating parameters.
  c. Stress the importance of the job.
  d. Take time to communicate effectively.

6. Follow-Up
  a. Insist on timely information.
  b. Act promptly and appropriately.
  c. Insist on results, but not perfection.
  d. Encourage independence.
  e. Learn to live with differences.
  f. Don't short-circuit or snatch back assignments.
  g. Reward good performance.

Note: From Merrill E. Douglass, *The Time Management Workbook* (Grandville, Mich.: Time Management Center, 1979), p. 60. Copyright 1979 by Dr. Merrill E. Douglass, Time Management Center. Reprinted by permission.

is expanded upon with substatements or questions. The guidelines are readily adaptable to education. They can be applied to the simplest or the most sophisticated assignments.

Human Resources Available to Teachers

Teachers have available to them a significant pool of prospective assistants. Many would be willing to give of their time and talents if they were asked. Students and school personnel respond to requests as a part of the team. Out-of-school citizens often feel that they have expertise to offer. They desire to be identified closely with the school in some capacity.

The kinds and number of human resources available to teachers for special assignments are as great as the teacher's imagination. Within the school are students, other teachers, librarians, counselors, nurses, administrators, secretaries, custodians, and others who can be tapped for doing a broad range of tasks. Such out-of-school groups as parents, government employees, and service club members have contributions to make. For example, the vocational school agriculture teacher with vision makes use of farmers and ranchers, farm implement dealers, seed dealers, nurserymen, bankers, lawyers, insurance agents, foresters, county agricultural agents, soil conservationists, and game wardens, to mention a few. These highly qualified specialists may speak in classes or club meetings, serve on advisory committees, sponsor educational activities and events, recommend training stations for students, donate instructional equipment and materials, prepare judging teams, and fund demonstration projects.

What to Delegate

From the pool of potential assistants just enumerated, four groups have been selected to illustrate the variety of tasks that may be delegated by teachers. In the lists that follow, review the tasks that may be delegated, respectively, to students, student teachers, teacher's aides, and advisory committee members. With the understanding that school law, local policy, personnel contracts, and general conditions differ among schools and states, ascertain the tasks that teachers would be permitted to delegate in your school system.

Depending upon state school law and board of education policy, the teacher may have *students*

Delegation

- Serve as aides during special school programs
- Be safety officers in laboratory or on playground
- Operate mimeograph machine
- Be in charge of supply room or school store
- Make in-school deliveries
- Draft articles for school newspaper
- Clean and maintain instructional tools and equipment
- Set up and operate audiovisual equipment
- Prepare drafts of thank-you letters to sponsors or awards programs
- Check attendance or roll
- Plan meeting agendas (club officers)
- Provide clerical assistance (business education student)
- Write and address own postcards announcing a summer activity or event
- Gather data for class project or classroom research
- Do housekeeping chores—organize furniture and pick up paper from floor
- Grade selected papers and tests
- Keep club scrapbook and records
- Be official department photographer
- Help plan some aspects of instruction
- Evaluate teaching

Under the careful supervision of the cooperating teacher, *student teachers* can

- Prepare and teach lessons
- Prepare and administer tests
- Score tests and record grades
- Assist with classroom management
- Prepare teaching materials
- Manage school laboratory or shop
- Assist in ordering school supplies
- Inventory community resources available to school
- Recommend books and materials for library
- Maintain a clean and attractive classroom
- Assist with study hall, playground duty
- Help with student club or cocurricular activities
- Provide remedial help to selected students
- Arrange and conduct a field trip
- Help prepare reports

- Write newspaper article
- Review homework papers
- Counsel students with academic problems
- Evaluate student progress
- Evaluate effectiveness of instructional materials
- Evaluate course or program

Tasks appropriate for *teacher's aides* have been defined in the U.S. Department of Labor's *Dictionary of Occupational Titles* (1977). (Let local job descriptions for teacher's aides guide assignments, however.)

Teacher Aide 099.327-010

- Prepare lesson outline and plan for review.
- Plan, prepare, and develop various teaching aids such as bibliographies, charts, and graphs.
- Present subject matter to students.
- Prepare, give, and grade examinations.
- Assist students, individually or in groups, with lesson assignments.
- May confer with parents on progress of students. (p. 72)

Teacher Aide II (Clerical) 249.367-074

- Call roll and prepare attendance records.
- Grade homework and objective examinations.
- Distribute teaching materials to students.
- Keep order in the classroom, library, school grounds.
- Set up and operate audio-visual equipment.
- Prepare requisitions for materials and supplies.
- May type or operate duplicating equipment to reproduce instructional materials. (p. 203)

"An advisory committee is a group composed primarily of individuals outside the educational profession who are selected from segments of the community collectively to advise educational personnel regarding one or more educational programs or aspects of a program" (Cochran, 1980, p. 4). The following tasks (conceived more in terms of a vocational education program than an academic or general education program) can appropriately be delegated to an *advisory committee*. The committee may be asked to

- Assist in short- and long-range planning
- Communicate work-related information to the school
- Review program goals and objectives for relevancy
- Assist in identifying guest speakers

- Recommend new equipment for programs
- Locate cooperative education training sites
- Assist in preparation of program improvement proposals
- Provide assistance in development of good community public relations
- Arrange for resource teachers from industry to assist regular teachers
- Obtain needed school equipment and supplies on loan or as special gifts
- Arrange field trips for students and teachers
- Sponsor educational competitions, contests, and scholarships
- Assist in development and review of course content
- Evaluate physical conditions, adequacy of equipment, and layout of laboratory or shop
- Assist staff with evaluating quality of program

Develop lists of tasks that can be delegated to other individuals and groups in the school and community. Some general rules are to delegate.

- Only those tasks that have been clearly defined
- Tasks that are challenging and rewarding
- Tasks suited to the abilities of the individual
- Those tasks that others can do better and more quickly than you
- Such tasks as fact finding, preparation of drafts, performance of routines, clerical work, and general housekeeping

To fail to use all available human resources to the fullest in education is a tremendous waste. Symptoms of poor delegation may include a bulging briefcase and extended workdays and weeks for the teacher, an obsolete course of study, lack of program and personal priorities, dated records, and disorganized instruction. Delegation is at its best when the instructional program is rated superior and the teacher has adequate time to plan ahead and make relevant changes without infringing upon personal time.

Closing Statement

It is probable that the teacher who cannot delegate effectively cannot manage instruction effectively. Delegation is a managerial technique for using other peoples' time. It is a way of sharing tasks and assignments. Delegating tasks, however, does not relieve the teacher of the ultimate responsibility associated with the delegated task.

Some teachers delegate readily, while others are most reluctant to do so. Those who delegate, and do it judiciously, appreciate the advantages. Delegation provides teachers time for planning and evaluation, so critical to instruction, without dipping into personal time; it offers the delegatees rewarding opportunities and challenges; and it is a way for teachers to promote more comprehensive programs of higher-quality education at no greater cost of professional time.

Teachers should view delegation as an integral part of teaching. The numbers and kinds of tasks that can be delegated are impressive. The numbers and kinds of people who are qualified and willing to be of assistance or assume assignments are unbelievable. Teachers who make the effort to match those assignments that need to be done with people who want to do them stand to reap tremendous benefits for both themselves and their schools.

7
Saying Yes or No

> Of all the time-saving techniques ever developed, perhaps the most effective is the frequent use of the word *no*.
> —Edwin C. Bliss

The myriad requests for a teacher's time require yes or no answers. The answers are bound to influence future behavior of both the requester and the teacher. Yet many, and perhaps most, yes or no answers are the result of spontaneous reactions rather than weighed decisions. Before you draw any conclusions about a request or give an answer, make sure that you clearly understand the request and have weighed it in terms of your own goals, priorities, schedules, and values. Is the request on target, or is it a digression? Making the decision is easier when guidelines have been established. If the request is complicated or delicate, you may need to ask for additional information and more time before saying yes or no.

It is generally acknowledged that teachers are conditioned not to say no to requests relating to their professional work. They are trained to provide a social service under time constraints and a host of institutional directives. The amount of work associated with teaching is endless: the quality of output eludes exacting measurement. As a result, teachers are not sure when nor how well they have satisfied requirements and expectations of, and obligations to, students, parents, administrators, and board members, among others. One urge is to overcompensate for the condition—to do more, to give additional time. The nature of the position causes the teacher to tend toward yes responses to requests. It is said that this characteristic spills over into the personal lives of teachers. Teachers, it would appear, give more than their fair share of time to others.

Saying Yes

To quote Rutherford (1981), "One reality of time is that it is never totally your own. You must share it with others with whom you work, live and interact" (p. 171). Saying yes is accommodating to the appeals of others; it is a matter of compromising your own time. It is easier to say yes than deny a request; following through can be more painful. Be cautioned that whenever you say yes to others, you are saying no to yourself. However, sharing your time, with all its ramifications and consequences, is a personal prerogative. Bowing to persuasion can result in an activity that will cause you much mental anguish over the waste of time. If a commitment causes you unhappiness later, perhaps the decision to say yes was not the best.

There are many reasons why people give freely of their time. Some are valid; many are indefensible. It is generally acceptable to say yes to an invitation when (1) you want to participate, (2) the activity is important to you, (3) the project moves you toward your goals, or (4) the assignment is part of the contracted job or a defined social role. A range of additional reasons why people say yes are that they

- Are afraid to say no
- Want to be popular
- Want to make others feel good
- Get ego satisfaction from being needed
- Want to appear positive
- Are paying a debt
- Have not learned how to say no

Which of the above reasons can you defend? Which cause you to answer positively when you do not want to? Human relations and values play a part in reaching decisions about requests for your time.

The consequences of saying yes should preferably be dealt with during the decision-making process. Query your own feelings. Ask yourself, for example,

- Do I have mixed feelings or resentment about the answer I'm intending to give?
- Could someone else do this task just as well or better?
- Does it involve potential stress or health problems?
- How much will my own personal goals be delayed or advanced?

The consequences of saying yes can be, and often are, more painful than giving a negative response would have been. The point is that when the answer is yes and time is committed, the experience should be satisfying, rewarding, challenging, and exciting. If it is not anticipated to be so, why submit to the request?

Saying No

Saying no to a request is often a tough thing to do. Children are taught not to say no. Such precepts as cooperation, service, and duty are written into creeds and philosophies of school youth organizations. Coaches encourage teamwork; they strive to develop positive attitudes. The democratic way of life encourages youth to do things and be somebody. Those steeped in this kind of training often express feelings of guilt, selfishness, and worthlessness when later in life they reach a decision to say no.

A more recent trend is in the direction of individualism—a doctrine that puts your interests above those of others. The belief associated with this movement is that "my time is my time." In this case saying no can be a positive action. A bill of assertive rights by Smith (1975) proclaims, "You have the right to say no, without feeling guilty." Furthermore, "You have the right to offer no reasons or excuses for justifying your behavior" (inside front cover). A rash of books are attuned to individualism. They focus on "you" and details on "how" to be successful, improve practices and procedures, and overcome deficiencies and weaknesses. As a result of the emphasis on the awareness of self, saying no is being done more, with less agony. In fact the assertive would say that they have a right to feel good about decisions to say no.

WHEN TO SAY NO

The conditions for saying no can be established. Being aware of these conditions can be a valuable aid in arriving at firm answers quickly—a definite advantage in convincing others not to attempt to change your decision. Say no when

- The request does not get you closer to your own goals
- It is questionable whether you can deliver
- Pressure is exerted for an immediate answer
- You just do not want to do it

- You are overcommitted
- The function is ethically or morally repugnant
- Other choices and options are more promising

Scott's prescription for learning to say no when you want to depends upon increasing

Your self-respect
Your confidence about relying on your own standards and decisions
Your comfort about meeting your own needs
Your recognition that you are not responsible for others' feelings
Your understanding that your worth does not depend on other people's judgments
Your comfort and confidence in pleasing yourself (1980, p. 207)

Is it unreasonable to say no when a request works against established plans, when it is expected to be burdensome or overwhelming, and when it is likely to inflict hardship or conflict with personal values? In the quest to use time advantageously, is it not better to chance erring on the side of saying no than to yield to time-consuming and peripheral activities? The judgments are yours to make; the resulting consequences are yours to endure or enjoy, whichever they may be.

HOW TO SAY NO

Say no tactfully but firmly. Be prompt, courteous, and pleasant, but persistent in the exchange. Guard against making excuses, wavering, expressing regrets, qualifying decisions, offending, and arguments. The first step in the process is to listen intently to ensure a full understanding of the dimensions of the request. Next, respond to the request in such a way as to eliminate all doubts about your decision. Finally, anticipate a reaction when the answer is "no," but move toward closure.

WAYS OF SAYING NO

Saying no to a request can range from forceful to very weak replies. The response is dependent upon the language selected and the style in which it is delivered. Examples of a range of responses follow:

"No" or "The answer is no" are two forceful responses when communicated in a convincing way. The simple word "no," presented as a statement of intention, is a complete message. The way it is communicated can strengthen the response. The gesture of shaking the head "no" further reinforces the position. "The answer is no" is a full and concise statement that emphasizes firmness. Both of the answers are to the point and understandable. Neither allows for verbal maneuvering. Any reaction to either answer can be countered by repeating the answer. The response "The answer is still no" can be added for variety.

Modifying "no" responses weakens answers. Giving reasons and offering suggestions open the door for discussion and a possible reconsideration of the "no" answer. If the urge is to explain, give an honest reason, state previous plans or schedule, or suggest the name of someone else who is qualified and might be anxious to be involved. Start the modified no response with "no." Follow with the explanation. Short sentences and answers are best: for example, "No, I have tickets to the concert that night" or "The answer is no. I'll be on vacation. You may want to call the Speakers Bureau. The number is 765-4321." If you try, you can win most of the time with a modified no.

The conditional "no" response to a request amounts to a "maybe" and is only a step removed from saying "yes." It is followed by alternatives to demonstrate a reserved willingness to be accommodating. Through a kind of negotiation, a compromise, trade-off, or deal is made. The plan of action is to (1) learn the details of the request, (2) clarify your own wants in relation to the request, and (3) explore creative ways of satisfying both the request and your own needs. "No, I won't be able to favor your request unless . . . because . . . or until . . ." opens the way for discussion of alternatives and options. The conditions bargained for may be an exchange of work assignments, access to special resources, or compensatory time, to name a few. The conditional "no" response to requests is profitable for those who negotiate well. The tactic tends to discourage subsequent requests.

Examples of very weak responses to requests are "I had thought about shopping tomorrow night, so I had better say no" or "I have never done that kind of work before, so I'd better not try it." A weak response to a request is apt to come from those without plans and goals for using their time or training and experience in saying no. They have no just cause or they do not know how to say no forcefully. They react to the stimulus of the moment; they hesitate, waver, and send mixed signals of indecision when tapped for their free time. Delayed, weak responses allow the requester to redirect strategy, work on emotions, and increase the pressure. When trapped in a weakened position, you generally emerge a loser. As a result, another someone has taken a chunk of your time and a piece of your life.

PRACTICE SAYING NO

If you find it difficult to say no when you want to, practice until you become more skillful at the task. Respond to simulated situations. Draft a number of reasonable answers to a request. Practice delivering the answers orally. Find styles that feel comfortable, and adapt them as necessary. You may have to be assertive on occasion in responding to a request. Figure 7.1 is an exercise in saying no that

FIGURE 7.1. Exercise in Saying No

Your ability to say no when you want to will improve with practice. Three situations follow. Each requires a different kind of "no" response. Respond to each question. Compare your responses to the sample answers in figure 7.2.

Situation 1. You are attending a faculty education meeting and have been unexpectedly nominated from the floor for the position of president of the Education Association. Although flattered, you must say no. How will you say no gracefully but forcefully to your peers?

Situation 2. A community organization for handicapped children has requested that you, a vocational teacher with a wealth of practical skills, teach a class of these children for twelve Saturday mornings during the summer months. This is not what you wish to do during your vacation. How would you say no tactfully, using the response technique for a "modified no"?

Situation 3. You, a classroom teacher, have received a call to report to the principal's office. The principal asks you to accept the position of acting chairperson of your department. The chair was vacated earlier in the morning and will not be filled permanently until the beginning of the next academic year. You know you do not really want the acting position, but what kind of conditional no can you give to the principal?

you can use for practice. Read and analyze each of the three situations for seeking some of your time. Assume that your answer is to be "no"; what is your response to each of the situations? Next, compare your answers with the sample answers and comments in figure 7.2.

Have mental crutches handy for those occasions when you are about to waver. Keep a list of carefully prepared "no" responses near the telephone to guide you through tough situations. Secondly, draft a number of self-contained paragraphs that say no in different forms. The sample paragraphs inserted into letters save time in two ways. They reduce the amount of time normally needed to compose the letter, and they deny a request for an unspecified further quantity of your time.

Respect for Your Time

One final thought is worth mentioning. Getting others to respect your time reduces significantly the number and kinds of requests made of you. You may be in demand because you possess precious skills, do high-quality work, and deliver on appointed times. These are desirable traits; do not attempt to change them. On the other hand, you may be in demand because you appear to have the time, are readily available, and work for free. These latter behaviors tell others you have little respect for your own time.

Before you can get others to respect your time, you must first respect your own time. Deliberate demeanor and candid exchanges with others are useful means of bringing about change in them. Here is a sampling of behaviors that may influence others to have more respect for your time:

- Evidence a busy schedule by limiting chats in the hall, visiting in the lounge, and lingering over lunch.
- Make it a practice in meetings to move quickly from small talk to the business at hand.
- Move deliberately and with purpose as you pursue work and leisure.
- Have something along to do while waiting for a ride or appointment. Read a book, or plan for tomorrow.
- Be organized. Manage classroom and personal affairs in a businesslike way.

FIGURE 7.2. Answers to Exercise in Saying No

Situation 1

Answer: "Mr. President, I respectfully decline the nomination."

Comments: Respectfully declining a nomination in a business meeting is a courteous and humble, yet forceful, way of saying no. The response does not need an explanation when one is nominated from the floor as a surprise move. This response does not allow for verbal maneuvering.

Situation 2

Answer: "The answer is no. While I am sympathetic to your needs, the request is too demanding."

Comments: The answer "no" preceded the explanation. This is a good start. Next, the response was stated somewhat tactfully. Being sympathetic with the cause aligns you with the organization, but at what expense in time? Twelve Saturday mornings during the summer vacation is a lot of precious weekend time. The request is absolutely too demanding; the answer is a truthful one. Finally, the brevity of the explanation allows little time for the requester to formulate a reaction. The chances of winning this one are good.

Situation 3

Answer: "No, but thanks for the consideration. As you know, my teaching load is the heaviest in the department. The position of acting chairperson carries with it limited benefits. Accepting it would slow my progress toward the master of education degree in educational administration. Since we're at the midpoint in the school year, I am not aware of any possible trade-offs that could make the position acceptable to me."

Comments: The answer was "no," but it was cushioned. The three short statements that followed the negative response reported present conditions, appealed for information, and presented goals. The teacher was thinking "out loud." The open response gave the principal feedback to use in exploring alternatives beneficial to both parties. Depending on further discussion, the outcome may be a more forceful "no" or a "yes," with the conditions negotiated for the acting position possibly being superior to the ones the teacher presently encounters as a classroom teacher.

- Use an appointment book. Be punctual, and expect others to be on time also.
- Be assertive in trade-offs and deals when others make requests of you. Shrewd trade-offs quickly convey the concept that your time is a valuable resource.
- Discourage interruptions. They are often the most common and most costly time-wasters in schools where population density is high.

Managing yourself to use time well, whether in school or elsewhere, just has to rub off on at least some of those with whom you associate. If you respect your use of time, others also may learn to respect your use of time. It follows that they may be a bit more hesitant about imposing on you, especially if they are not managing themselves to use their own time at a similar or higher level of efficiency. Set a positive example. The first move is yours.

Closing Statement

The process of arriving at answers to requests for some of your time can range from automatic responses to painstaking decisions. Drawing the line between "yes" and "no" is a sensitive and complex exercise that is crucial to the success of teachers as managers of instruction and to individuals as masters of their own lives.

Saying yes to others means sharing or giving a portion of your time. The consequences of overgenerosity and unwise decisions can cause emotional discontent, mental anguish, and stress. Be selective. Opportunities are unlimited; time is not.

Teachers have a right to say no without feeling selfish about their use of time. Saying no to requests that infringe on instructional activities or that could adversely affect your physical health or temperament, for example, can make you a better teacher. Professional time is still your time to use, and enough of it cannot be had to favor all requests. It is only reasonable and natural that some requests for your professional and personal time cannot be answered in the affirmative.

When the activity is repugnant, say no to the request. The bitterness of following through can remain long after the sweetness of saying yes is forgotten. The decisions to give or withhold your time are yours to make; but you must live with the consequences.

8
Wasting Time

> I have but one life and life is naught but a measurement of time. When I waste one I destroy the other.
>
> —Og Mandino

We all waste time. Some of us waste more time than others. Occasionally we waste time intentionally; more often it is done unwillingly or unconsciously. Time is a resource that cannot be manipulated. It is *always*, but *only*, available for use in the present. How well present time is used is measured somewhere on the efficiency-inefficiency continuum. A *time-waster* is an activity that keeps you from achieving your objectives. Didactics Systems (*Managing time effectively*, 1977) suggests that "one of the best ways to reduce the amount of time you waste is to periodically ask yourself the question, Am I using my time in the best possible way, right now? If the answer is 'no' you are probably wasting time and not focusing on one of your top priorities" (p. 39).

Identifying Time-wasters

The ways to waste time are numerous. Some are obvious, while others are more difficult to define, since they depend somewhat on circumstances. For example, daydreaming can be considered to be a time-waster in one situation and defended as a kind of productive creativity in another. Delaying a decision is usually thought of as a time-waster, but there are occasions when a delayed decision is a time-saver. Perhaps when so-called time-wasters are done with purpose, they really are not time-wasters.

Figure 8.1 is a partial list of potential time-wasters categorized into clusters. The intent of the list is to acquaint you with the kinds and numbers of time-wasters readily at hand to rob you of productive minutes, hours, and days. The instrument can be used to identify your worst time-wasters as a first step in formulating a plan for using your time better.

Classroom Time-wasters

A specialized cluster of teacher time-wasters in the classroom could have been added to the list in figure 8.1. These include

- Calling roll
- Disciplining students
- Hunting lost teaching aids
- Condoning poor furniture arrangements
- Using unreliable audiovisual equipment
- Socializing during instructional time
- Using obsolete instructional resources
- Providing irrelevant instruction
- Teaching lessons without preparation
- Competing against distractions
- Spoon-feeding students facts
- Teaching when students aren't ready to learn
- Beginning a job and not completing it.

The reverse of a time-waster, whether in the classroom or not, is a so-called time-saver. Eliminating time-wasters and using time well simultaneously is a powerful "one-two" punch in any time use self-management program. Time-savers—efficient time users—are reviewed fully in the next chapter.

Dealing with Time-wasters

Baker (1979) explains how time-wasters are generated:

> Time wasters may be internally generated by you or externally generated by events or other people. Internally generated time wasters are the easier ones to resolve because they stem from your own actions or inactions. Thus, if you are part of the problem, you

FIGURE 8.1. Potential Time-wasters

The time-wasters listed below are categorized into clusters. For each cluster, assess your own strengths and weaknesses by ranking your top three strengths A, B, and C and your bottom three weaknesses X, Y, and Z. Congratulate yourself on the strengths. Use the weaknesses as the foundation for an improvement plan.

Potential Time-wasters	Strengths (A-B-C)	Weaknesses (X-Y-Z)
Affective Components		
Forgetfulness	____	____
Indolence	____	____
Indecision	____	____
Aimlessness	____	____
Tactlessness	____	____
Daydreaming	____	____
Lack of motivation	____	____
Managerial Concerns		
Unclear objectives and goals	____	____
Lack of priorities	____	____
Poor scheduling	____	____
Too many interests	____	____
Clutter/disorganization	____	____
Failure to plan	____	____
Doing the wrong thing	____	____
Energy Drainers		
Stress/tension	____	____
Worry	____	____
Low morale/blues	____	____
Frustration	____	____
Impatience	____	____
Fear	____	____
Illness	____	____
External Factors		
Drop-in visitors	____	____
Telephone interruptions	____	____
Meetings	____	____
Waiting	____	____
Commuting/travel	____	____
Excessive paperwork	____	____
Red tape	____	____
Personal Hangups		
Failure to listen	____	____
Ineffective communication	____	____
Lack of knowledge and/or skills	____	____
Excessive attention to detail/perfectionism	____	____

FIGURE 8.1 (continued)

Potential Time-wasters	Strengths (A-B-C)	Weaknesses (X-Y-Z)
Doing things over/sloppy work	_____	_____
Saying yes too often	_____	_____
Hopping from task to task	_____	_____
Doing it myself	_____	_____
Procrastination	_____	_____

can become part of the solution. Time problems which are externally generated, however, require more imagination and creativity because they are not totally within your control. (p. 3)

EXTERNALLY IMPOSED TIME-WASTERS

A category of time-wasters that requires very attentive, special judgment is contractually imposed time obligations. School law, teachers' contracts, and board policies specify activities that keep teachers from achieving their own instructional objectives or using their own professional time in the best possible way. By definition, they are time-wasters; relative to the professional's position, they are time obligations. For example, attendance at three or four teachers' meetings per school year may be acknowledged as an obligation when one signs a contract. Contractually, additional teachers' meetings are not time obligations. In retrospect, attendance at the required meetings could have been time-wasters as well as time obligations. Hopefully, attendance at all meetings, including additional ones, was time well invested.

Such time obligations as reporting to school fifteen minutes prior to the first class and remaining for another fifteen minutes after the school day is ended, participating in school "open house" activities, keeping extraordinary records, and preparing special reports are frequently viewed by teachers as time-wasters. Administrators make the requests because the activities are required or because they are viewed as beneficial to the school. When time obligations imposed by administrators conflict with professional goals of the teacher, the time obligations are given priority. Two alternatives that teachers have to accepting time obligations are to effect change through proper channels and procedures or resign the position.

External time-wasters, those imposed by other people or events, may be "drop-in" visitors, incoming telephone calls, meetings you are expected to attend, waiting for others or for transportation, red tape, and numerous other happenings or demands. They are more difficult to deal with than internally generated time-wasters in that an outside influence has been introduced.

Probably two of the most demanding externally imposed time-wasters confronted by teachers are waiting for others, and "drop-in" visitors. Realizing that teachers are professional public servants trained to accommodate the needs of others, here are some model tactics for dealing with waiting and drop-in visitors.

1. *Waiting.* One must wait for public transportation. Waiting in line, getting stuck in traffic, being put on hold while telephoning are other examples. Time spent waiting seems forever. When waiting, fight frustration by reading, doing mental planning, or striking up a meaningful conversation if possible. To quote Thomas Edison, "Everything comes to him who hustles while he waits." Carry a project to work on while being forced to wait.
2. *Drop-in visitors.* The tactic is to reduce visiting time or discourage the practice altogether. When the unannounced visitor drops in, stand up and move toward the intruder. The technique reduces visiting time immeasurably. Remain standing, but get down to business. Ascertain the purpose of the visit. Answer the request, or, if it will take more time, set up an appointment. If the visitor continues to linger, conclude with a statement such as, "I'm sorry; I can't talk any longer. I have an appointment waiting [a class to teach; a report to get out]." Remember: "The man who has taken your time recognizes no debt, yet it is the only debt he can never repay" (Papyrus).

Interruptions are common external time-wasters that can be considered a part of the job of teaching. Many, and possibly most, are unnecessary. Figure 8.2 lists a number of instructional interruptions with which teachers commonly deal. Try to develop strategies for minimizing time wastage for a sampling of the interruptions. For example, answer incoming telephone calls, unless emergencies, after class; carry extra bulbs with projectors for quick replacement when one burns out; and provide students with meaningful, purposeful instruction to reduce or eliminate disciplinary problems.

FIGURE 8.2. Instructional Interruptions and Their Control

Interruptions are time-wasters. Some can be expected as a part of the instructional process. All must be curbed. If callousness is justifiable at all in teaching, then it surely must be in the control of interruptions.

Instructions: From your experience, add to the open-ended list of interruptions. Next, underline several of the worst offenders and develop strategies for minimizing the wasting of time in your instructional setting. Try out the strategies for effectiveness.

1. Fire drills
2. Assembly programs
3. Overused public address system
4. Mid-morning physical examinations for athletes
5. Incoming telephone calls
6. Late-arriving students
7. Accidents in shop or laboratory
8. Bulbs burned out in projectors
9. Student horseplay
10. An unusual occurrence such as a snowstorm
11. Running out of chalk in the middle of class
12. A picture on the wall falls to the floor
13. Arrival of a visitor at the classroom door
14. _____
15. _____

INTERNALLY GENERATED TIME-WASTERS

Perhaps all potential time-wasters on the list cited in figure 8.1, except those in the cluster on external factors, are generated internally and must be dealt with through your own actions. When you have identified your own internally generated time-wasters, you are aware of the areas over which you have had limited control but that you potentially can master. This accomplished, the next step is to devise personalized tactics for dealing positively with each time-waster. The plan can be as simple or as complicated as deemed necessary to gain control. Some sample tactics for dealing with several of the internally generated time-wasters listed in figure 8.1 follow.

1. *Forgetfulness.* Counter forgetfulness with aids for remembering. Prepare and use a daily list of things to do. Keep a pocket or desk appointment book. Write each item down immediately, and refer

to these notes on a regular basis. The reward for remembering is getting each activity done on time and striking it off the list.
2. *Indecision.* Understand that indecision is a form of procrastination. There are no riskless decisions, and bad ones may be better than no decisions. Be aware that delay does not necessarily improve the quality of decisions; it does result in stressful crisis management. The logical answer is to get the critical facts and make an early decision. The bonus is that early decisions allow time for adjustments.
3. *Unclear objectives.* For suggestions on clarifying your objectives, see the section entitled "Goals, Objectives, Priorities" in chapter 2 ("Managing Yourself").
4. *Doing things over.* Doing things over is a waste of time. The causes of unacceptable work can be mistakes, lack of information, carelessness, misunderstanding, haste, or poor communication. Excuses also waste time; instead, spend the time on salvaging poor actions or unacceptable work. Set acceptable standards for output, and stick by them. Learn from setbacks.
5. *Worry.* Worry is mental distress that takes much energy. It is unproductive and actually counterproductive. Do not worry about eventualities over which you have no control, but do not ignore them either. "Our main task is not to see what lies dimly perceived in the future, but to do the thing which lies immediately ahead," wrote Thomas Carlyle.
6. *Hopping from task to task.* This may be a sign of overcommitment or a means for keeping ahead, but it is costly of time. Determine your priorities for the day. Start with the most important task. After it is finished or can go no further for the day, go on to priority number two, and so forth. The answer is to do a task to the finish. When one thing is dropped to finish another, you have interrupted yourself. Complete tasks before you put them down. Otherwise you must refamiliarize yourself with the task when you return to it. Don't confuse being busy with being effective.
7. *Doing it myself.* See chapter 6, "Delegation."

Procrastination

Procrastination is singled out for special attention, since it appears to be the most universal and costly of all internally generated time-wasters.

Procrastination is a palatable word for such distasteful behavior as "putting off" or stalling unnecessarily. The practice is commonly referred to as a disease, bad habit, or laziness. In essence, procrastination is delaying until later what is uncomfortable to do at the moment. Everyone does it on occasion; some do it regularly.

Teachers, by the very nature of their professional position, must be self-starters. Needless delays not only affect teachers but usually affect students adversely as well. The rule is to delay the activity only if it keeps you from a higher-priority activity. It is easy to ignore the rule, but doing so is a step toward becoming infected by or addicted to the procrastination syndrome.

REASONS FOR DELAYING

To become familiar with the underlying reasons for procrastination is progress in the direction of correcting the time-waster or avoiding the pitfall. Several authors have explored the reasons for putting things off, and their combined insights and perspectives present a comprehensive view of the causes underlying the problem.

Knaus (1979) lists and describes five basic reasons for delays:

1. Physical Incapacitation—When one has severe medical problems that serve to stop him or her from proceeding.
2. Ignorance—When a person doesn't realize a deed needs doing.
3. Stratagem—Developing an awareness of the job's priorities. Some delays are strategic.
4. Discomfort Dodging—When any unpleasant but important activity is avoided because the person wants to avoid hassle. . . . The task is put off because some parts of it are associated with uncomfortable, possibly anxious, feelings.
5. Self-doubt—When a person judges his abilities as questionable and defines his adequacy as a person on the basis of these questionable qualities. . . . Normally, a more intensely negative self-view is closely associated with hesitating and delaying.

Knaus hastily notes that "the delays due to physical causes, ignorance, or strategy are understood and accepted." His book stresses discomfort dodging and self-doubt as causes of "needless delays that interfere with both psychological growth and the smooth administration of life's details" (pp. 4–7).[1]

---

[1] Excerpts from the book, DO IT NOW by Dr. William J. Knaus. © 1979 by Prentice-Hall, Inc. Published by Prentice-Hall, Inc., Englewood Cliffs, NJ 07632. Reprinted by permission.

Why do we procrastinate? Lee (1980) lists seven basic reasons:

1. [The activity] seems too time consuming.
2. It's a long range project.
3. [It's not of] immediate importance to you.
4. You haven't made a commitment.
5. Doing it now will be unpleasant.
6. You don't have a deadline.
7. You see no immediate profit.

Lee's summary is that "these are all the wrong reasons for delaying. If you delay something for these reasons, you are wasting time. This kind of delay is very definitely negative" (pp. 74-75).

"Most but not all reasons for procrastinating are emotional in nature," wrote LeBoeuf (1979), in introducing his list of reasons why we put things off. The emotional reasons are

To escape an overwhelming task
To excuse poor work
To gain sympathy
To get someone else to do the job
To protect a weak self-image
To avoid change (p. 119)

The nonemotional reasons for procrastinating mentioned by LeBoeuf are improper goals, insufficient information, goals without deadlines, overcommitment, and unrealistic time estimates.

HOW PROCRASTINATION WASTES TIME

Stalling is not using time in the best way possible at the moment it is available. The activity that should be done now is put aside in favor of another with lower or no priority for achieving stated goals. Delaying the completion of a high-priority activity indicates that time is being spent carelessly or used less productively—both wasters of time.

A second way that procrastination wastes time is through undermining one's emotional and physical health. Through nagging guilt, self-disgust, worry, and hopelessness, putting things off has a way of draining one emotionally. Pressures, stress, and fatigue resulting from stalling take a measure of the procrastinator's physical health.

Putting things off compounds the wasting of time. The price paid for wasting time by procrastinating is cumulative, and it is doubly costly. When uncontrolled, procrastination can quickly ruin a career, a marriage, and a life.

CORRECTING THE PROBLEM

The major reasons for procrastinating are emotional problems, poor health and physical disorders, and self-managerial dysfunction. To correct the problem, you must rescue yourself. The suggestions that follow can help you deal with diagnosed frailties.

1. *Assess health.* Keep healthy by eating wholesome food, getting adequate sleep and rest, and engaging in an exercising program. Schedule physical examinations with a physician on a regular basis. People with energy and vitality get things done—on time. Illness, infirmities, and pain have a tendency to slow down activity, but they need not make a procrastinator out of a person. Feeling well is a qualitative judgment, but most people know when they are well and when they are not. If involvement in an activity causes one to become sleepy, get a headache, or just feel awful when there is no apparent reason, search for one anyway. The symptoms associated with the activity have a delaying effect and are counterproductive.
2. *Observe emotions.* Uncomfortable feelings, for example, are associated with unpleasant, overwhelming, and rushed tasks. Anger, fear, frustration, worry, and other emotional stressors can stall or stop a project. Lack of ability causes delay; lack of skill to perform causes hesitation. There is a tendency to put off indefinitely tasks that one finds difficult to do or that on previous occasions ended in failure. Procrastination thrives on emotional blocks. When possible, match tasks with temperament and ability, but also be courageous and flexible enough to attempt new and challenging tasks occasionally.
3. *Review work load.* If you are recognized as an outstanding teacher who cannot say no to any request or delegate anything to anyone, chances are that your work load is heavy, staggering, or impossible. The consequences of too much to do are (1) overwork, (2) reduced quality of output, (3) a backlog of undone tasks, or (4) all of the above. If none of the consequences is acceptable and if your goal is to continue to be an outstanding teacher, the work load must be adjusted. You may choose to say no to some requests, delegate more tasks, or resort to the full bag of aids to efficient time use. The aim is to keep the work load manageable and to

prevent backlogs that ultimately lead to procrastination. Meet your goals, but do it on terms that are more just and fair to you in this game of life.
4. *Analyze habits.* Are you chronically late in arriving at school, meetings, and appointments? Do you more than occasionally receive second notices to submit reports and pay bills? Are you inclined to watch television at the expense of doing pressing tasks? Do you usually hold on to journal articles and research proposals that you are writing, for the sole purpose of making them perfect? If so, habits of procrastination have been formed or are developing. The obnoxious thing about being late is that it affects others who are waiting, writing follow-up letters and memos, and making excuses on behalf of the tardy individual. Teachers who have the habit of being late put pressure on administrators, colleagues, students, family, and friends. Their lateness strains relationships. Regardless, it has been said of some that the habit is so ingrained that they will be late for their own funerals. Some suggestions on correcting the problem are given in the section on habit control in chapter 2.
5. *Consider the worth of activities.* Some tasks are superb ways in which to invest time; some are not worth doing; most range somewhere between the two extremes. The difficulty is to impress upon yourself which are which. To quote Lin Yutang, "Besides the noble art of getting things done, there is a noble art of leaving things undone. The wisdom of life consists in the elimination of nonessentials." Weigh the worth of future activities in terms of your present goals and priorities. Do those *few* things that are vital; cast aside those *many* things that are trivial. Indecision about the worth of an activity leads to procrastination. Reach a decision, and let that decision be known. When positive, it generates momentum to follow through; when negative, it informs others of the position taken.
6. *Schedule activities.* Scheduling is the linking of activities you plan to do with time frames in which to do them. Time, until scheduled, is an unfilled dimension; conceived activity, until scheduled, is a fantasy at the mercy of caprice and whimsy. The marriage of time to proposed activity—scheduling—is a format for commitment. Appointment calendars and "to do" lists cue one to follow through and be punctual. Both are effective if you (1) are motivated to do the things listed and (2) do not schedule too much too tightly. A balance between commitment to your goals and willingness to meet your obligations to others keeps the schedule stimulating. In

preparing schedules, consider your own strengths and weaknesses, likes and dislikes. Finally, when activities are complicated or overwhelming in scope, set aside large blocks of uninterrupted time in which to do them. If this is not possible, restructure the difficult and time-consuming activity to fit smaller increments of time that are available. If you want things to happen, arrange the components so that they can and will happen—on schedule.
7. *Follow through.* Do it now. A slow start makes a task more arduous. An ancient proverb advises, "He has half the deed done, who has made a beginning." At the start, however, understand fully the scope and complexity of the task at hand. Too many are inclined to provide the answer before they analyze the question, to see individual pieces without envisioning the whole, or to solve problems by trial and error at the expense of the logical thought process. Each is wasteful of time. Each delays the successful completion of the task. If necessary, restructure the task into manageable parts. Do the easy parts first, if getting started seems to be a problem. If lack of motivation is a factor, do parts that you do well. Give the task "prime time" to get it going. Keep it going when the ideas are flowing, morale is high, or the pieces are fitting together well. It is exhilarating to finish ahead of time; it is humiliating to be late.

REWARD PUNCTUALITY

If you finish ahead of the designated time, acknowledge this achievement to yourself. Strike the task off the list of things to do. Celebrate the occasion by treating yourself to a special dinner, buying the new pair of shoes you have looked at so often in the store window, or purchasing tickets to your favorite sports events. The reward does not need to be costly to reinforce the new habit, just as long as it makes you feel good about yourself and your modified behavior. Try it. It works.

Closing Statement

While time is free and ever-present, it is not a resource one can afford to waste. Some people waste more of it than others. Time is wasted when it is not used in the best possible way. The best possible way to spend time is in achieving established goals and objectives.

Time-wasters are robbers not easily identified. They use minutes, hours, and days with returns that are meager at best. They steal time in different ways, and many are habitual offenders. Know the ones that are taking advantage of you, and be determined to control them.

Time-wasters are imposed by others or yourself. In dealing with time-wasters that others intend to force upon you, be comfortable with the position that it is justifiable for teachers to guard against the abuse of their personal and professional time. The internally generated time-wasters stem from your own actions or inactions. The cause of the problem points to you, and you are the one appointed to solve it. Each acknowledged internally generated time-waster can be dealt with through individualized self-prescribed regimens, which when practiced faithfully replace the unwanted behavior.

Delaying until later what is uncomfortable to do at the moment is a time-waster that usually has emotional roots. The malady touches every life at one time or another. Confessing the problem and desiring to do something about it must precede treatment if the treatment is to be successful. Be positive in your approach to dealing with the tendency to unnecessarily delay and to be late. Counter with the time use suggestions for correcting the problem proposed in this chapter. Reward yourself for being punctual. It helps entrench the desired behavior, and it makes you feel good.

9
Time-savers

> All that time is lost which might be better employed.
> —Rousseau

Time cannot be saved. *Time-saver*, a commonly used term, is a misnomer. A time-saver, in reality, is an efficient or effective *time user*. Saving time, then, is getting more out of the time that is yours to use.

The words *efficient* and *effective* are usually used together in time management literature, although they have quite different meanings and serve two distinct purposes in managing oneself or others to use time well. LeBoeuf, a management expert who specializes in organizational behavior and communications, distinguishes between the two words as follows:

> All too often, many of us confuse effectiveness with efficiency. Being effective is choosing the right goals from a set of alternatives and reaching them. Efficiency, on the other hand, assumes the goals as given and proper and proceeds to find the best means of achieving them. Efficiency is doing the job right, whereas effectiveness is doing the right job. In a nutshell, effectiveness means results. Both are valuable concepts, but in my mind, effectiveness is far more important. (1979, p. 9)

Bliss, a specialist in problems of time management, sums up the meanings of the two words this way:

> Efficiency concerns the best ways of doing an assigned job. Effectiveness, on the other hand, concerns the *best use of time*—which may or may not include doing the particular job in question. . . . Sound

time management involves thinking in terms of effectiveness first and efficiency second. (1976, pp. 32-33)

Douglass (1979) distinguishes between the two words in one sentence: "Efficiency concerns doing the job right, while effectiveness requires doing the right job right" (p. 13).

Doing the Right Things: Effectiveness

Decisions to let certain things go undone are just as important as decisions to do certain other things. Busywork, marginal projects, and non-goal-oriented activities should be recognized as such and deliberately avoided. Effectiveness is saying no to unreasonable requests; eliminating unnecessary filing of papers; and canceling regular business meetings when there is no business to transact. It is giving precedence to high-priority activities.

Master teachers are acknowledged effective professionals who do not try to do everything. They make it a practice to spend time in proportion to the gain anticipated. Making the best use of time by doing the right things leads to the road of success. Experience, sound judgment, and a sense of values, coupled with a wholesome attitude about the use of time, are qualities that help to make teachers effective.

Doing Things Right: Efficiency

After decisions are made on what is to be done, discharging the responsibility comes to the forefront. Efficiency means to perform with the least waste of time or, stated positively, with the best use of time. While doing an assignment may require a number of resources in varying amounts, it is the resource of time that is of concern here. Particular strategies and methods can be learned that will help teachers to be more productive and hold the cost of their time to a minimum.

The ways and means of doing things efficiently are virtually endless in number. In time management literature, time-savers— efficient time users—are usually presented in the form of a list of statements. Sometimes each time-saver is followed by an explanation. The simple listing of behaviors acquaints the reader with the range of methods of doing things more efficiently, while the explanation usually explains the "how" and "why" for a time-saver.

A list of categorized time-savers for teachers is given in figure 9.1. The time-savers are listed without any or with little interpretation. Some are self-evident, and some require a little thought. A more detailed discussion of some of them (those marked with an asterisk) is given in the following section of this chapter ("Twenty-one Time-savers").

Try using this list in a number of ways. You may question why or how each statement qualifies for the list. Having done this, you may want to mark the time-savers that you would be inclined to adopt. You may also add your own items that the list has stimulated.

The next section examines the "why" and "how" of some of these time-savers. Before reading these explanations, you may want to mentally prepare your own reasons, for the purpose of comparison.

Twenty-one Time-savers

Just as there are myriad ways to use time to better advantage, so are there numerous ways to explain how or why particular time uses are efficient. The explanations are necessarily rather general because the situations involved may vary, and it is virtually impossible to address all contingencies. These general explanations are therefore conceived in the light of a collective set of beliefs, judgments, and circumstances that are not likely to exactly parallel many real-life situations. The test is to apply the interpretation to your very real situation. Try those that prove attractive and modify them, as necessary, for your own use. My hope is that you will adopt some new time-savers and learn how much they can add to your efficiency and effectiveness.

TEACHING

Use competency- or performance-based lessons or modules. Competency- or performance-based lessons or modules are written in behavioral terms. Behavioral objectives deal directly with learning essentials. They are statements of what is to be done, under what conditions it is to be done, and at what level of proficiency it is to be done. For example, suppose that this is the behavioral objective: given eight spark plugs, an operator's manual, and a feeler gauge, the student will be able to set the spark gap for each plug as specified (.025 inch) in the manual. The teacher knows precisely what is to be taught. Students know exactly what is to be learned. Both the teacher and

(continued on page 113)

FIGURE 9.1. Some Time-savers (Efficient Time Users) for Teachers

---

Teaching
Teach with the support of a lesson plan.
Peg instruction at a level that is understandable.
Concentrate on instructional clarity.
Use realia and visuals generously.
Employ supervised study, programmed instruction, and computer-assisted instruction.
Use mimeographed procedure sheets to minimize individualized instruction.
Give preference, when appropriate, to teaching groups over teaching individuals.
Take into account the reviewing and marking process when making homework assignments to students.
Use competency- or performance-based lessons or modules.*
Use answer sheets and other resources for scoring objective tests.*
Improve listening skills of self and students.
Control deviant behavior of students.*

Preparation and Planning
Have the resources needed to get the job done at school and at home.*
Be guided by updated courses of study with objectives that are realistic and measurable.
Reserve a quiet time each day for planning.
Use graphics to expedite instruction. *
Use lists of daily things to do.
Keep and use an appointment calendar.
Use abstract and clipping services.
Use "high-lighter" marking pens on your own printed materials such as books, reports, and memos.
Reduce an overpowering job to mere tasks.*
Make use of a wheeled cart to organize and move equipment, supplies, and instructional materials.*
Prepare the kinds of tests and examinations that accommodate to time constraints of the teacher and conditions of the job.*

Filing and Storing (Housekeeping)
Use color-coded folders or labels for quick identification of categories.
File only those items that are likely to be referred to at some future date.
Store files vertically rather than in piles, so that items can be recovered with a minimum of shuffling.
Keep working files near the desk.
Purge files of questionable content regularly and often.*
Store reusable stencils for future use.
Maintain a test question bank.*

---

*Asterisk identifies those time-savers on the list that are discussed in some detail in the section of this chapter entitled "Twenty-one Time-savers."

FIGURE 9.1 (continued)

Use carousel trays for organizing and storing two-by-two-inch slide presentations. Slides are always ready for use, in proper order, when permanently stored in trays.
Obtain and safeguard owner's (service) manual for machinery and equipment in the classroom and laboratory.*
Maintain a supply and equipment inventory on file cards or computer tape.
Lock storage cabinets and supply rooms.
Have a place for everything, and have everything in its place when it is not being used.

Meetings, Conferences, and Appointments
Know the purpose of a meeting, appointment, or conference before attending it.
Establish time limits for beginning and ending meetings, appointments, and conferences.
Use parliamentary procedure in conducting business meetings.
Capitalize on time spent waiting for a function, individual, or transportation.
Precede a visit by making a "firmed-up" appointment.
Know the location of a function or obtain directions for getting there before starting the journey.
Summarize from notes your understanding of outcomes of a conference or appointment to check accuracy and as one means of achieving closure.
Walk with lingering visitors toward the exit, at the end of an appointment.
Combine attendance at distant professional conferences that extend over a number of days with social functions and recreational activities.

Relations (Student, School, Community, Public)
Write short letters.
Use form letters with standard paragraphs for routine matters.
Write replies on margins of letters, and file a machine copy for future use.
Keep an assortment of special-occasion cards in your desk at school as well as at home.
Use preprinted order forms.
Throw junk mail in the wastebasket as soon as it is received.
Handle the bulk of the mail preferably only once.*
Keep a pad, and a pencil that writes, by the phone.
Group outgoing telephone calls.
Leave phone messages rather than call later.
Make use of the two-way intercom system in the school.
Discourage interruptions, especially during teaching and planning periods.
Keep short and to the point those interruptions that do happen.

FIGURE 9.1 (continued)

Adopt a regulated open-door policy.*
Make use of public media to inform large numbers of
   people.
Use school and program brochures generously.
Use business cards.*
Prepare presentations that can be used repeatedly with
   service clubs, civic organizations, and other groups.
Pay visits to persons who have records of prolonging
   visits when on your turf.
Put limits on your proposed service role in the commu-
   nity.

Supervision and Administration
Delegate to others; use a wide variety of assistants and
   helpers.
Encourage student independence in pursuing assignments.
Use written rules and regulations to characterize de-
   sirable student behavior in your classroom or labora-
   tory.
Have students keep their own permanent cumulative record
   folders maintained in the classroom files.
Request that problems brought to you be accompanied by
   some proposed solutions.
Share progress and problems with a course or program lay
   advisory committee.
Have adequate teaching aids and resource materials on
   hand.
Order consumable supplies in large amounts to avoid fre-
   quent reordering.
Have laboratory and audiovisual equipment in good work-
   ing condition.
Take the initiative.*
Follow teaching contract and job description guidelines.
Deal with problems when they surface.
Be fair and just in all dealings.

Personal
Have goals and objectives for self-direction.
Carry a pencil and supply of three-by-five-inch index
   cards on which to take notes.*
Benefit from your own computer system.
Prioritize items in lists according to importance.
Do it now; get started immediately.
Set deadlines.
Don't strive for perfection; know when to quit.*
Terminate activities when they become unproductive.*
Sharpen memory for recall.
Stop worrying.
Keep healthy.
Think before talking and writing.
Reside near school.
Put things away while they are in your possession.

FIGURE 9.1 (continued)

Practice safety.
Rise early.
Walk faster.
Synchronize activities with your biological time clock.
Know where your time goes.
Earn respect for your particular attention to the use of time.*
Plan and schedule rest periods and vacations.*
Rethink life at every stage to get the most out of it.

Note: Portions of this figure are adapted from J. Christiansen, Time Saving Techniques, Department of Agricultural Education bulletin no. 80-1 (College Station, Tex.: Texas A & M University, 1980), pp. 11, 13, 15-20, 25, 28, 30, 32-34; E. B. Feldman, How to Use Your Time to Get Things Done (New York: Frederick Fells, 1968), pp. 68, 162; and A. Lakein, How to Get Control of Your Time and Your Life (Bergenfield, N.J.: New American Library, 1973), pp. 159-160.

the learner know when the teaching and learning process is complete and the standard has been achieved.

The very same behavioral objective used in the lesson is also the test criterion. Test preparation is not necessary. The criteria for grading are more often objective than subjective. Scoring can be done quickly, and the feedback is immediate.

The teacher who uses performance-based modules serves as a resource person or manager of instruction in the learning environment. In these capacities it is often possible to do other tasks besides meeting student needs. The nature of the position allows for broadened activity by the teacher.

Use answer sheets and other resources for scoring of objective tests. Test booklets not written on can be used again and again. Used with objective tests, single-page answer sheets take less time to hand score than a multiple-page test with answers on the margin of each page. Page flipping is eliminated.

Mechanical aids permit faster scoring of answer sheets than hand scoring. One suggestion is to make a scoring key. To do this, mark the correct answers on one copy of the answer sheets. Paste a backing on it for durability. Punch out the correct answers. Use the key as an overlay to score the students' answer sheets.

Another suggestion is to score answer sheets by machine when the equipment is on site and the questions are of the multiple choice or true-false types. Test-scoring machines are inexpensive, and they are simple to use. (1) Have students record answers with a no. 2 pencil on a prescribed answer sheet. (2) Mark a similar answer sheet with correct answers, and feed it into the machine to program it for scoring the test. (3) Feed students' answer sheets into the machine for scoring and to obtain the number of correct answers for each student.

On occasion have students score each others' answer sheets under your supervision. In addition to saving time, the exercise provides students with an additional learning experience. They also receive immediate feedback in the form of seeing what the correct answers are, when the procedure is done properly.

Control deviant behavior of students. Deviancies are distractions. They disrupt and delay teachers and teaching. The teacher who disciplines in a highly emotional way adds to the distraction, disruption, and delay. When behavior is controlled, the time saved can be added to instructional time.

Students need structure and direction in the learning setting. They want a rationally ordered instructional environment. They appreciate a firm but fair teacher. They respond positively to meaningful and purposeful instruction presented enthusiastically.

Work in positive ways to shape student behavior. Managerially, know what is going on, establish set routines, remove temptations, reduce frustrations, define limits, and make the connection between behaviors exhibited and consequences. Pedagogically, begin class promptly, make transitions from one activity to another smoothly, use a variety of teaching methods and techniques, minimize teacher talk, focus on learning by doing, and make clarity of communications a priority in teaching and making assignments.

Prevention or control of deviant behavior is a good investment of teacher time. Disciplining can be and often is a costly user of time, and especially so when stress-related factors are added to the cost.

PREPARATION AND PLANNING

Have the resources needed to get the job done at school and at home. The list of resources at the desk or home office falls into three categories: supplies, tools and equipment, and special items. When all are available as needed, time can be saved in doing the task.

Inexpensive desk supplies do tend to disappear. Staples, paper clips, transparent tape, and pencils are used up and borrowed without notice. Especially at school, take an inventory and obtain necessary supplies before settling at the desk to do the job. One trip to the supply room before starting the job is a more efficient use of time than several trips made while at the job. Also, fewer trips are less stressful. To make sure that you will have desk supplies when you need them, store them, including extras, in a locked desk drawer. The added advantage of this practice is that the desk top is at least partially cleared and ready for action.

The tool and equipment list should include, but not be limited to, a dictionary, a thesaurus, directories, professional journals, and books, as well as a telephone, typewriter, and calculator. Each in its own way is intended to be an aid and time-saver for the user. Acquire such additional things as drafting equipment, a camera, and a tape recorder if they reduce work time or make it more exciting.

Special items relate to specific projects and activities. They can be file folders that hold reports, records, or minutes. They can be forms to fill out, questionnaires to complete, or mail to answer. It is not unusual for these special items to be in school when you are at home, or vice versa. A work schedule, a reminder, and a briefcase with the special items in it will save an extra trip to pick them up so that work can proceed.

Use graphics to expedite instruction. A one-page picture, map, diagram, chart, or graph can often be substituted well for many pages of wordy descriptions and explanations. Graphics should be put together in such a way that the parts as well as the whole can be observed simultaneously. The finished product can be a slide, wall chart, overhead transparency, or mimeographed handout. Graphics are readily available from commercial suppliers. They also can often be produced by teacher and students rather quickly.

Turn to graphics to accelerate understanding and bring about agreement. For example, students know without asking questions where they stand in relation to others by referring to the skills chart on the wall. Maps accurately pinpoint locations of cities, rivers, and roads. Pictures capture actuality; they are efficient means of keeping certain kinds of records.

Graphics, through directness of expression, simplify teaching and heighten learning. They sell ideas, and products for that matter, when time to do so is restricted.

Reduce an overpowering job to mere tasks. Simply stated, an occupation is made up of a cluster of jobs; a job is made up of a cluster of tasks. A task is an individually distinct unit of work that consists of logical steps, has a starting and a finishing point, and is performed in a relatively short period of time. In essence, a task is a miniaturized unit of work that in itself has meaning. On occasion a job appears so imposing or so complex that one is reluctant to tackle it. Then, as we have seen, a common reaction is to procrastinate. The solution is to analyze the job and reduce it to smaller tasks, thus dividing and conquering the seemingly insurmountable job.

Tasks are more manageable than jobs. They can be scheduled to use small segments of time. Also, tasks are easier to delegate than jobs because they are less complicated. Finally, having the option to elect easy tasks first stimulates one to get started. A substantial start is often motivation enough to finish the remainder of the tasks and, consequently, the job.

Make use of a wheeled cart to organize and move equipment, supplies, and instructional materials. The cart is kind of an organizer, in one sense, and a silent workhorse in another. It is usually made of metal and has three shelves mounted on four wheels, two of which swivel. It can be rolled with ease from office to classroom or laboratory on smooth floors.

Teachers with carts have an added advantage over those without carts. Those with carts can

- Use brief periods of free time for loading the carts in preparation for instruction
- Take a quick inventory of items grouped on them, which more than occasionally saves steps in returning for something that was forgotten
- Handle loads on one trip that might otherwise require two or three trips
- Use the top shelf as a desk or stand for setting up projection equipment

The equipment cart is especially useful to teachers who teach in a number of classrooms and to laboratory instructors who use large amounts of equipment and supplies in their teaching. Once accustomed to having a cart, it is burdensome to do without one.

Prepare the kinds of tests and examinations that accommodate to time constraints of the teacher and conditions of the job. More teacher time is required to *prepare* an objective test than an equally comprehensive essay test, but less teacher time is required to *grade* the objective test than the essay test. The busy teacher faced with a test date will be wise to prepare a test that will not require too much time to prepare. If a test is administered the day before report cards are due, for example, and no other considerations are involved in the decision, the teacher is encouraged to select an objective test to avoid a last-minute rush in grading.

Putting aside all other considerations, the teacher who meets small classes can save time by preparing and grading *essay* tests, whereas the teacher who meets large classes can save time by preparing and grading *objective* tests. The point on the continuum from small to large classes where the kind of test is no longer a time-saver for the teacher varies with test writing conditions and grading services.

FILING AND STORING (HOUSEKEEPING)

Purge folders and files of questionable content regularly and often. There is a tendency to keep everything because it may be needed someday. One result is a full and, in many instances, a packed set of files. You will know it is time to clean out the files (1) at your first impulse to purchase additional filing cabinets; (2) when folders are stuffed, faded, bent, and in disarray; and (3) when a mountain of materials is waiting to be filed but you feel that fighting the bulging files to do the job is just too aggravating and costly of time.

One reason why people tend to put off cleaning out files is because they must decide what to cull and what to keep. Once the job is tackled, it is not as difficult or time-consuming as often supposed. Teachers know which materials are needed for future reference. Throw old catalogs and directories in the trash can. Transfer graduates' folders and dated reports to the inactive file. When you are finished, the active folders should be thin; the files should have ample space for receiving useful references.

Why are purged files time-savers? There are three reasons:

- Empty space makes filing quick and easy.
- Retrieval is fast. There are fewer materials to search; there is less chance of lost items; and when located, the items are easy to remove.
- Filing is more spontaneous. The items are put where they belong immediately. They can be recovered more readily from a file than when hidden somewhere in a horizontal pile.

Be cognizant of the fact that when selectivity is practiced in initial filing, purging needs to be done less often later.

Maintain a test question bank. Writing an examination can consume a sizeable block of time. Rummaging through examinations administered previously to find usable test items is not the best use of time. Access to a test question bank reduces the time needed to prepare an examination, makes the task more exciting, and the resultant product will probably be better.

What is the procedure? Accumulate a bank of test items from previous examinations, through an exchange arrangement with other teachers, from purchased materials, and by personally creating items as a result of instructional outcomes. Write, paste, or tape questions onto four-by-six-inch index cards for uniformity and ease of handling. File the cards by such categories as subject matter, unit of instruction, and lesson. Continue to add questions or items to the bank as an ongoing project.

When a new examination is needed, first determine the length and content. Next pull the desired number of relevant questions from the bank, sequence them, and have a secretary or teacher's aide type them into a test format and make the necessary number of copies.

Granted that building the bank takes time, the earlier it is done and the more use made of it the greater will be the time advantage gained. The time gained in examination construction can be used in such evaluation activities as doing an index of item difficulty for each question and determining the reliability coefficient for the examination. It is conceivable making such validity and reliability assessments could save time later that is taken up by disputes with students over the fairness of test items and examinations.

Obtain and safeguard the owner's (service) manual for instructional machinery and equipment used in the classroom and laboratory. It has been quipped that the owner's manual is often estimated to be worth half of the purchase price of the piece of equipment. While not in itself a costly item, the owner's manual is valued highly as a time-saver by those who (1) want to learn how to use the equipment, (2) are expected to maintain and repair the equipment, and (3) order replacement parts.

Owner's manuals differ in content, but they all offer useful time-savers such as safety precautions and warnings about use; assembly, installation, and operating instructions; specifications and performance data; maintenance care; trouble checklists for diagnostic purposes; and directions on how to order replacement parts, with lists including the names and numbers of parts. Avoiding an accident, using efficient operating procedures, preventing breakdowns, and doing your own troubleshooting are potential time-savers encouraged by owner's manuals.

Vocational teachers often use owner's manuals as instructional and learning resources. The practice saves time over ordering similar kinds of materials.

RELATIONS (STUDENT, SCHOOL, COMMUNITY, PUBLIC)

Handle the bulk of the mail preferably only once. Mail is not something to read and then lay aside after your initial curiosity is satisfied. Returning to opened mail means reading it again and other lost motion before taking action.

On the first handling of mail, one of three actions is suggested for each piece: put it in a wastebasket, respond to it immediately, or lay it aside. Specifically,

1. Dispose of junk mail immediately by putting it in the wastebasket or through a paper shredder.
2. Respond on first handling to information pieces and routine items. If it survived the wastebasket, respond to it: post dates of forthcoming events; pen a thank you note or congratulations on an all-purpose card; follow up a request with a telephone call or by jotting it on your "to do" list; reroute a catalog to another interested person or file it for future reference. As noted earlier, you can save time in answering letters by hand writing short, legible replies directly on the letter received and returning it to the writer.
3. Limit severely the amount of mail put aside for a second perusal. Valid reasons for putting it aside may be the need for additional information; lengthy, technical reading; or other extenuating circumstances. The usual guide is that 20 percent or less mail should be handled a second time.

Do something with a piece of mail while it is in your hand and the message is fresh in your mind. Actions 1 and 2 save time. Action 3 cannot be avoided, but it can be controlled. To put mail on a pile to be shuffled, reread, and possibly reread again is not a time-saver.

Adopt a regulated open-door policy. An open-door policy means different things to different people. It may or may not mean that the door is ajar. It may or may not mean that everyone is privileged to walk in at any time. Keeping an open-door policy may mean that you are regarded as a good teacher or not a good teacher.

In the past, administrators often looked with disapproval at a closed-door policy because schools are public institutions that are people- and service-oriented. On the other hand, constant interruptions can be devastating to the teacher and the instructional program. It is a rare occasion when someone drops by to save the teacher time by volunteering help or services. People tend to come by to request assistance, socialize, or for some other unexplained reason. Whether the purpose of the visit is genuine or not, all visits take teacher time.

To control entrance through the office or classroom door, establish management practices.

1. Locate the office away from the mainstream of traffic, if possible. An out-of-the-way location reduces calls because of inconvenience. It also reduces "drop-in" inquiries about directions to another part of the building.
2. Limit seating accommodations in the office. Inadequate accommodations discourage the use of your office for socializing and meetings.
3. Keep the door closed. An open door is an invitation to enter; the closed door requires a knock. Answer the knock with a question. "Do you have an appointment?" "May I help you?" To say "Come in" may be an invitation costly of time.
4. Have a "quiet time" posted when interruptions are frowned upon. Be stern enough to make the management practice work.

Use business cards. The use of business cards means that you have available for others attractive "on-the-spot" information about yourself and the school at which you are employed. The card carries with it a clue to personal organization, a stripe of the professional, and a flair of distinction. It is more efficient and more rewarding to give a personalized business card than it is to find a scrap of paper, hold it against the wall, and scribble on it your name, address, and telephone number with questionable legibility. The scrap of paper does not have the lasting value a business card has in the hand or pocket of another.

How can business cards be used as time-savers? (1) When at an exhibitors' show, use a business card to request a book from a publisher. It saves time filling out the request form. (2) Answer a request for a handout or reprint of a journal article by sending it with a business card attached. It saves writing a cover letter. (3) When in a group that is exchanging business cards, you had better have some. It saves time explaining. Business cards make satisfactory bookmarkers, emergency note cards, and luggage identification when they are sandwiched between plastic sheets. The initial contact, without a further investment of time, could activate a consultancy, a new job opportunity, or some other exciting adventure in life.

Put limits on your proposed service role in the community. Distinguish between community service and public school education. Service to a community is a contribution to the welfare of others. Education deals with teaching and learning in the school. Since education is service-oriented, it can be construed to spill over into the community service area as well.

There is a continuous search in communities for people to be of service in one way or another. The need is for people to direct projects, coach teams, manage playgrounds, provide leadership, make presentations, teach Sunday school, serve as scout leaders, and more. Teachers have the training and ability to perform well in all of these civic, social, and religious responsibilities and are frequently called upon to do so.

As worthy as they may be, good turns and helpful acts take time. While community service is not a part of the job, teachers commonly agree that it should be allotted some of their time. The debatable question is how much time. The answer is that each teacher has to establish a limit and a policy. To avoid becoming a slave to community service activities, know when to say no. A community service overload can adversely affect the quality of your teaching in school and your family relations at home; a balanced and controlled community service program can be most beneficial to both. Pick and choose the kinds of service activities that help you meet your own goals and objectives. Limit the number of activities accordingly.

SUPERVISION AND ADMINISTRATION

Take the initiative. Reputation is often made on the ability to get things done. Take it off the shelf; set the stage; get the wheels turning. Invest time by taking action; waste time by delaying action. Taking the initiative gives one a time advantage.

Attach conditions to requests for responses from others. For example, "If no comments are received by [date], the memo, as written, will be circulated." Or, "If you do not arrive by [time], I'll start the meeting with the assumption that you will be absent." Waiting wastes time; initiative can trim waiting time.

Seize opportunities. At business meetings, speak to motions on the floor. In professional associations, assume leadership responsibility. Announce your preferences prior to or at the time assignments are being made. Take advantage of the situation. Doing anything less can result in waste of time.

PERSONAL TIME-SAVERS

Carry a pencil and a supply of three-by-five-inch index cards on which to take notes. Write on cards the notes that are likely to be needed later. Names and addresses, factual data, and dates of upcoming activities can be forgotten readily. Less time is required to pick up the information from a card in your own possession than to procure it from someone else. It is also conceivable that if you are in the habit of interrupting others, they feel free to interrupt you.

Record seemingly bright ideas as they occur to you. To capture an idea on paper is a more efficient use of time than to let it slip back into the subconscious mind and hope for recall later. Ideas on cards, usable parts of a puzzle, may form the nucleus for some creative thinking at a later time: two or more bright ideas may be fused into a major breakthrough or an incredible discovery.

Write down things that need to be done at designated times. Jot them down rather than forget about them. Forgetfulness requires excuses and apologies that are not productive users of time. A short pencil is a better time-saver than a long memory.

Don't strive for perfection; know when to quit. Behavioral phenomena are so complex and instrumentation so crude that a precise way of measuring perfection is somewhere in the distant future. Tasks that educators perform do not demand perfection. However, statistical reports should be accurate; lesson plans should be complete; and grammar should be correct. All smack of perfecton. So does excellence, which is a more widely used term than perfection among educators. Excellence has a degree of qualitative latitude that perfection does not.

Knowing when to stop investing time in a project or activity saves the resource for some other purpose. If you are already achieving excellence or near-excellence, putting in additional time can give diminishing returns. In attempting to achieve excellence, time is the expandable variable, while quality of output is fixed. It is possible that a standard may be set at an unattainable level.

A decision to "improve it" or "let it go" must be made at some point along the way about each project. What is the grade average that a class must achieve before you are satisfied with the quality of your instruction? How much supplementary reading is necessary to understand a concept? Are all possible references required for an excellent bibliography? Decisions in favor of excellence may be influenced by fear of failure or demands by superordinates; decisions against excellence may be forced by a pending due date. Excellence takes additional time, while something less than excellence gives additional time. Know when to quit.

Terminate activities when they become unproductive. In a business meeting, when a motion has been discussed fully, move the previous question. Take a vote after a reasonable amount of discussion, and especially when discussion is not relevant to the motion.

In the classroom, encourage lively discussion, but when a discussion reaches its zenith, summarize the major points made and move on to another learning activity.

In school, avoid the daily exchange of smalltalk. Keep conversations on a professional level with colleagues and at the instructional level with students. The school is the work place of the teacher.

On the telephone, when the purpose of the call has been satisfied, express gratitude and hang up. It is not rude to do so; it is the way a businesslike transaction is completed.

During an appointment, stay on the topic. When the objectives are met, signal the end of the conference by standing. Shake hands, if it is the custom, and depart or prepare for the next activity, depending on whether you were guest or host.

Earn respect for your particular attention to the use of your time. Teachers who pay particular attention to how well they use time have purpose, are organized, and possess plans that help them to be high achievers. In striving to get the most out of time, their behavior in this regard is different from that of the average teacher. On occasion they may be viewed as quaint or strange. They may be more frequently talked about than regarded as models, but in either case their associates have become aware that they view time as a precious commodity. Instilling such awareness is an important step in the process of gaining respect.

Consider it an invaluable time-saver when others demonstrate respect for your concern about the wise use of time. This becomes evident when fewer requests are made for your time, but more so when the nature of the requests change and are supported by reasoned thought rather than made on impulse. Respect is evidenced when a measure of reasonableness accompanies a request for your time. Respect for your time can be presumed when possible solutions are presented along with a problem; proposed activities and appointments are arranged around your interests and goals; and resources and trade-offs are offered along with a request. Such considerations reduce time demands for doing the job, focus on challenging activities, and fit into or otherwise augment your plans. They are built-in efficiencies that manifest respect for your time. The bottom line for you is improved productivity.

Plan and schedule rest periods and vacations. Along the way, find refreshing paths that lead away from the working world, and use them when you need to. Take time for renewal of body, mind, and soul. Schedule time to live the fuller life.

But in what sense are rest periods and vacations time-savers? Time spent away from work influences efficiency of time at work. Extended periods without sleep and many hours of labor without rest adversely affect quantity and quality of work. Recesses during the day and vacations during the year are times set aside for rejuvenation. Just as they refresh students, so do they reinvigorate teachers. It follows that both teachers and students should be better achievers after than before the break period or vacation.

Closing Statement

A time-saver is, in reality, an efficient time user. Some people search for ways of doing things more directly and more quickly than by the ordinary procedure without sacrificing quality. Those who discover more direct routes to reaching goals have an urge to pass the ideas on to others. Time-savers for teachers, although not usually described as such, are more than occasionally recorded in the voluminous and diverse sources of pedagogical literature.

For the creative and innovative, the number of efficient time users (time-savers) is as great as the imagination will permit it to be. Time spent to contrive and implement your own time-savers or search for and adopt those of others can in itself be an efficient use of time. To quote Lord Avery, "It is not so much the hours that tell, as the way we use them. Life must be measured rather in depth than by length; by thought of action rather than by time."

10
The Challenge

If you have been interested enough in improving your use of time to read this far in this book, you have already taken the first step toward managing yourself to better use time. The next step, a giant one and the main challenge you face, is to put into practice a plan for improvement. A few words of encouragement from time management specialists are offered next, in the hope that they will encourage you to make the transition from reading to doing. Each excerpt has a sage message; when taken together and internalized, they pack the punch to surmount the challenge.

The simple fact that you have a strong wish to improve your use of time can help you succeed in the enterprise, according to McCay (1959):

> The key to success in anything, as you know, is *desire*. You must have a passionate desire to develop your resources. Everything you do must become a servant of this desire. . . . No matter what the level of your ability, you have more potential than you can ever fully develop in a lifetime. Regardless of your formal education, experience, position or age, it is never too late to start on the adventure of managing your time. (p. 166)[1]

Feldman (1968) assures us that time management skills develop quickly with practice:

> It has been said that the longest journey begins with a single step. Make your beginning, be sure you are on solid ground by repetition and review, and maintain steady acceleration. Associate with

---

[1] From the book, THE MANAGEMENT OF TIME by James T. McCay. © 1959 by Prentice-Hall, Inc. Published by Prentice-Hall, Inc., Englewood Cliffs, NJ 07632. Reprinted by permission.

doers and thinkers. Make stimulating contacts. Read. Expose yourself to the arts, those distillations of creativity and expression. Work at it. Before long it will be habit. You'll like the results. (pp. 270-71)

LeBoeuf (1979) stresses persistence in sticking to goals:

Effective people have an intelligent type of persistence. They realize that most of us waste our time and energy by abandoning our goals too soon. Once these people attach themselves to a dream, they hang on for the ride and enjoy every minute of it. . . . Working smart isn't a fantasy, but a reality within the grasp of all those who choose to reach for it. (pp. 224-25)

Ferner (1980) cautions us not to go too far in adopting time management practices. He writes:

The basic objective of time management is not to become super-efficient, super-productive, or super-busy, but to use our time in ways to achieve important personal goals. . . . As you manage your time, keep asking yourself, "Is this advancing my important goals?" or "Is this really what I want to be doing with my time?" (p. 204)

And Love (1981) describes the ultimate reward of learning to use your time well:

Eventually, you will find that you have mastered time. No longer will it be your master. You will know what your purposes are; you will have a priorities list; and you will guide your activities by those things that contribute most to your objectives. You will also know clearly what you want to do. . . . When you are master of your time, you will feel good about it. You will want to share your time mastery secrets with others—and you will have time to do it! (pp. 273-74)[2]

Time measures the length of life; use of time largely determines the quality of life. The ability to manage yourself to use time effectively and efficiently can move you to greater heights professionally and in other aspects of your life. Life can be filled with a continuous

---

[2]From the book, MASTERY AND MANAGEMENT OF TIME by Sydney F. Love, © 1978 by Sydney F. Love. Published by Prentice-Hall, Inc., Englewood Cliffs, NJ 07632. Reprinted by permission.

stream of fruitful activities and meaningful events, or it can be wasted on passive existence. In large measure, your life will be what you make of it.

The challenge is to seize the opportunity to invest your time in the best possible way. Begin now. Time waits for no one.

References

American Association of Agricultural College Editors. (1976). *Communications handbook.* Danville, Ill.: Interstate Printers and Publishers.

Arlin, M. (1979). Teacher transitions can disrupt time flow in classrooms. *American Educational Research Journal, 16,* 53.

Baker, H. (1979). *Techniques of time management.* Washington, D.C.: U.S. Government Printing Office.

Bartholomew, B., & Gardner, S. (1982). *Status of the American public school, 1980-81.* Washington, D.C.: National Education Association.

Berne, E. (1976). *The games people play.* New York: Ballantine Books.

Be somebody—Do something useful, grow the best that's in you. (1941). Chicago: International Harvester Co.

Beyer, B. K. (1971). *Inquiries in the social studies classroom: A strategy for teaching.* Columbus, Ohio: Charles E. Merrill.

Bliss, E. C. (1976). *Getting things done: The ABC's of time management.* New York: Charles Scribner's Sons.

Christiansen, J. (1980). *Time saving techniques.* Department of Agricultural Education bulletin no. 80-1. College Station, Tex.: Texas A & M University.

Cochran, L. H., Phelps, L. A., & Cochran, L. L. (1980). *Advisory committees in action.* Boston: Allyn & Bacon.

Committee for the Study of Diffusion of Farm Practices. (1962). *Adoption of new farm ideas.* East Lansing: Michigan State University.

Cooperative State Research Service. (1965). True objectivity. *Agricultural Science Review, 3,* cover page.

Cuban, L. (1982). Persistent instruction: The high school classroom, 1900-1980. *Kappan, 64,* 117.

Dillon, R. D. (1981). The word in time management is "organization." *Agricultural Education Magazine, 53,* 4.

Douglass, M. E. (1979). *The time management workbook.* Grandville, Mich.: Time Management Center.

Dover, C. J. (1966). Listening: The missing link in communication. In S. Duker (Comp.), *Listening: Readings.* New York: Scarecrow Press.

Feldman, E. B. (1968). *How to use your time to get things done.* New York: Frederick Fells.

Fensterheim, H., & Baer, J. (1975). *Don't say yes when you want to say no.* New York: Dell.

Ferner, J. (1980). *Successful time management: A self-teaching guide.* New York: John Wiley & Sons.
Flanders, N. A. (1970). *Analyzing teacher behavior.* Reading, Mass.: Addison-Wesley.
Gellerman, S. W. (1960). *The uses of psychology in management.* New York: Collier Books.
Gephart, W. J., Strother, D. B., & Duckett, W. R. (Eds.). (1981, March). *Practical applications of research,* newsletter, Phi Delta Kappa Center on Evaluation, Development, and Research, 3, 3.
Gurevich, A. J. (1976). Time as a problem of cultural history. *Cultures and time.* Paris: UNESCO.
Harris, T. A. (1969). *I'm O.K., you're O.K.* New York: Avon Books.
Knaus, W. (1979). *Do it now: How to stop procrastination.* Englewood Cliffs, N.J.: Prentice-Hall.
Kozoll, C. E. (1982). *Time management for educators.* Bloomington, Ind.: Phi Delta Kappa Educational Foundation.
Lakein, A. (1973). *How to get control of your time and your life.* Bergenfield, N.J.: New American Library.
LeBoeuf, M. (1979). *Working smart: How to accomplish more in half the time.* New York: McGraw-Hill.
Lee, J., & Pierce, M. (1980). *Hour power.* Homewood, Ill.: Dow Jones-Irwin.
Long, F. (1967). *All about meetings: A practical guide.* Dobbs Ferry, N.Y.: Oceana Publications.
Lortie, D. C. (1975). *School teacher: A sociological study.* Chicago: University of Chicago Press.
Love, S. (1981). *Mastery and management of time.* Englewood Cliffs, N.J.: Prentice-Hall.
McCay, J. T. (1959). *The management of time.* Englewood Cliffs, N.J.: Prentice-Hall.
McConkey, D. D. (1974). *No-nonsense delegation.* New York: AMACOM.
Machlowitz, M. (1980). *Workaholics: Living with them, working with them.* New York: Mentor, New American Library.
Mackenzie, A., & Waldo, K. C. (1981). *About time: A woman's guide to time management.* New York: McGraw-Hill.
Mackenzie, R. A. (1972). *The time trap.* New York: McGraw-Hill.
Mackenzie, R. A., & Lekan, D. (1977). Take a "quiet hour" for time to think and plan. *Training and Development Journal, 31,* 10.
Managing time effectively: A study unit. (1977). Cranford, N.J.: Didactic Systems, Inc.
Martinez, R. P., Zaino, W. J., Weger, C. D., & Collins, J. E. (1978). *Basic school law* (2 ed.), Trenton, N.J.: New Jersey School Boards Association.
Morgan, J. S. (1981). Apply communications wisdom. In C. H. Vervalin (Ed.), *Communication and the technical profession.* Houston, Tex.: Gulf.
National Education Association. (1980). *NEA research memo: Survey of NEA members.* Washington, D.C.: National Education Association.

References

National School Boards Association. (1982). *School personnel management system* (Locator 3.25). Washington, D.C.: National School Boards Association.

N.J.S.A. Title 18A:25-3 Education. *New Jersey statutes annotated*. St. Paul, Minn.: West.

Odiorne, G. S. (1980). *The effective executive's guide to successful goal setting*. A Special Management Report from MBO, Inc. Westfield, Mass.: MBO, Inc.

Owens, J. (1978). *Time management through transactional analysis*. Washington, D.C.: Management Education Ltd.

Pertrie, C. R., Jr. (1966). What is listening? In S. Duker (Comp.), *Listening: Readings*. New York: Scarecrow Press.

Roberts, H. M. (1970). *Robert's rules of order* (rev. ed.). Glenview, Ill.: Scott, Foresman.

Robinson, J. P. (1977). *How Americans use time*. New York: Praeger.

Rogers, E. (1962). *Diffusion of innovations*. New York: Free Press.

Rutherford, R. D. (1978). *Administrative time power*. Austin, Tex.: Learning Concepts.

Rutherford, R. D. (1981). *Just in time: Immediate help for the time-pressured*. New York: John Wiley & Sons.

Scott, D. (1980). *How to put more time in your life*. New York: New American Library.

Serif, M. (1961). *How to manage yourself*. New York: Cities Service Oil Co.

Shaw, H. (1945). *A complete course in freshman English*. New York: Harper & Brothers.

Smith, M. J. (1975). *When I say no I feel guilty*. New York: Bantam Books.

Steller, A. W. (1973). *Educational planning for educational success*. Bloomington, Ind.: Phi Delta Kappa Educational Foundation.

Sullivan, M. (1980). *Managing your time and money . . . : Strategies for success*. New York: American Express Co.

Thelen, H. A. (1960). *Education and the human quest*. New York: Harper & Brothers.

U.S. Department of Labor. (1966). *Training and reference manual for job analysis*. Bureau of Employment Security Publication no. E-3. Washington, D.C.: U.S. Government Printing Office.

U.S. Department of Labor. (1977). *Dictionary of occupational titles* (4th ed.). Washington, D.C.: U.S. Government Printing Office.

Voltaire, F. ([1749] 1974). *Zadig; or, The book of fate*. Reprint, edited by Michael F. Shugrue. (The Flowering of the Novel, 1740–1755, vol. 25). New York: Garland Publishing.

Webster's seventh new collegiate dictionary (1967). Springfield, Mass. G. & C. Merriam.

Index

Absence, leave of: extended, 45; temporary, 45
Administration, 112, 121
Advisory committee, delegation to, 82-83
Age, sensitivity to time and, 7-8
Agendas, planning meeting, 68
Annual reports, 59
Answer sheets, 113-14
Assistants, 77, 80, 81-82

Basic School Law (Martinez et al.), 34
Board of education, 33-34, 97
Business cards, 59, 120

Calendars, school, 33, 37-40, 124
Change strategy, 22-23
Channels of communication, 47, 49
Classroom: communication in, 54; control of behavior in, 114; terminating activities in, 123; time-wasters in, 95
Class schedules, 40-42
Clocks, 4-6
Community involvement, 44, 121
Competency-based modules, 109-13
Conferences, 41-42, 123; with drop-in visitors, 98, 119-20; time-savers for, 111
Contracts: in delegation, 77; teaching, 34-35, 42, 44-46, 97
Control: classroom, as time-saver, 114; through delegation, 76, 77; self-, 15
Correspondence, 58-59, 111, 119

Daily schedules, 40-42, 70-71
Dictionary of Occupational Titles, 35-36, 82
Discipline: classroom, 114; self-, 15
Drop-in visitors, 98, 119-20

Effectiveness, 107-9
Efficiency, 107-9
Emotions, procrastination and, 102, 103

Employment contracts, 34-35, 42, 44-46, 97
Equipment: carts for, 116; owner's manual for, 118
Examinations: answer sheets for, 113-14; question bank for, 59, 117-18; time constraints in, 116-17
Excellence, 122-23
Extracurricular activities, 42-43, 121

Filing, 110-11, 117-18
Following through, 105

Games People Play, The (Berne), 6, 20
Goals, 126; determination of, 15-17; priorities in, 18
Graphics, 115

Habits, 41; analyzing, 104; control of, 23-25; good listening, 60-62; reading, 56-57
Health maintenance, 103
Holidays, 33, 37-40
How to Put More Time in Your Life (Scott), 7-8

I'm O.K., You're O.K. (Harris), 20
Indecision, 94, 100
Index cards, 122
Innovation, 22-23
Instructional Clarity Checklist, 54
Interaction analysis, 63
Interruptions, 98-99, 111

Job descriptions, 35-37; teacher's aides, 82

Law, public school, 31-33; board of education enforcement of, 33-34; calendars in, 33, 37-40; teaching contracts in, 34-35, 42, 44-46, 97; time-wasters in, 97
Leadership, 42-44, 121

Leaves of absence, 44–46
Lecturing, 63
Lesson plans, 41, 63, 69
Libraries, 19
Listening, 60–62; good habits for, 60–62; pitfalls of comprehension in, 60

Mail, 58–59, 111, 119
Managerial tools, examples of, 18–28; change strategy, 22–23; habit control, 23–25; libraries, 19; time logs, 25–28; transactional analysis, 20–22; truth-seeking, 19–20
Maternity leave, 45
Meetings, 50–54, 64; conduct of business, 52–54; introducing speakers in, 51; planning agendas for, 68; preparation for, 51; time-savers for, 111
Memory joggers, 73, 99–100, 122
Messages, communication, 47, 49
Money, value of time in, 6–7

Nonteaching duties, 42–44, 121
Note-taking, 61–62

Objectives: establishment of, 17–18; priorities in, 18; unclear, 100
Objectivity, 20
Open-door policy, 119–20
Overcommitment, 100

Parliamentary law, 52–54
Perfectionism, 100, 122
Performance-based modules, 109–13
Personality: attitude toward innovation and, 22–23; use of time and, 13
Planning, 66–70; daily, 67–70; taking time for, 41–42, 67; time-savers in, 114–17. *See also* Scheduling
Priorities, 18; setting up, as time-saver, 100; in daily planning, 70; procrastination and, 104
Procrastination, 100–5; correction of, 103–5; indecision as, 94, 100; reasons for, 101–2; wasting time through 102–3
Professional involvement, 44, 45, 121
Programming. *See* Planning; Scheduling
Public school law. *See* Law, public school
Punctuality, 104, 105

Reading, 54–57
Receivers, communication, 47, 49
Recreation, 22, 124; time allocated to, 9–10; in time logs, 26

Requests: respect for your time and, 91–93, 123–24; saying no to, 87–91; saying yes to, 86–87
Research proposals, 68
Robert's Rules of Order, 52

Sabbatical leaves, 45–46
Scheduling, 70–74; to avoid procrastination, 104–5; daily, 40–42, 70–71. *See also* Planning
Self-control, 15
Self-discipline, 15
Sick leave, 44–45
Sleep, 9–10, 26, 124
Sources, communication, 47, 48–49
Storage, 110–11, 117–18
Stress, 12, 102–3
Students: classroom discipline for, 114; delegation to, 77, 80–81
Student teachers, delegation to, 81–82
Supervision, 112, 121

Talking, 62–63
Tasks, 115–16
Teacher's aides, 82
Telephone, 111, 123
Tenure, 39
Tickler files, 73, 99–100, 122
Time: characteristics of, 1–4; methods of measuring, 4–6; savers of, 107–24; as a scarce resource, 65–66; sensitivity to, 7–9; uses of, 9–11; value of, 6–7; wasters of, 94–106
Time logs, 25–28
Transactional analysis, 20–22
Truth-seeking, 19–20

U.S. Department of Labor, 35, 82

Vacation, 37–40, 124
Values: clarification of personal, 13–15; habits and, 25; impact on, of education, 19; saying no and, 87–88; saying yes and, 86–87; time use and, 10–11
Volunteers, 77, 80, 121

Waiting, 98
Work, 22; time allocated to, 9–11, 30–31; in time logs, 26
Workaholics, 15
Worry, 100
Writing, 57–60; rules and reference resources for, 58; time-savers in, 120; time-wasters in, 58–60

Zadig; or, The Book of Fate (Voltaire), 3, 29